THE LANDRY LEGACY

20 Principles of Success

Michael Thornton

Carpenter's Son Publishing

Acknowledgements

There were so many people who were instrumental in making this book a reality, individuals I would like to thank. First is George Andrie Jr for taking the time to call me back and put me in touch with his dad, George Andrie Sr, former defensive end of the Dallas Cowboys and one of the original members of the original "Doomsday Defense." Second is Wayne Lebaron for putting me in touch with his father Eddie Lebaron, the Dallas Cowboys first quaterback. Thanks to Eddie Lebaron who at 82 took time for me in between working out and playing a round of golf.

Thanks to D.D. Lewis and Tom Rafferty for taking the time to personally meet with me in the Dallas area. Each of these guys visited with me and encouraged me greatly.

Thanks to Donna Skell, Executive Director of Roaring Lambs Ministries. My wife introduced me to Donna and Donna introduced me to her boss Garry Kinder. As it turns out Garry and his brother Jack wrote a book with Roger Staubach in the early 80's. Garry graciously put me in touch with Roger Staubach. Both Donna and Garry helped me step by step to put this book together.

Roger Staubach described Garry Kinder as one the finest and rarest individuals he has ever met. Having spent time with Garry over the last couple of years I understand why. Garry consistently took time out of his busy schedule and partnered with me on this book. Every time I visited with Garry he always gave me at least one book, told me a handful of fascinating stories and shared a wealth of wisdom with me. Thank you Garry for your generosity and willingness to speek into my life.

Thank you Bill Krisher, who Garry also introduced me to. Bill helped me as much as anyone.

Thanks to Roger Staubach, Alicia Landry, Bob Lilly, Mike Ditka, Dan Reeves, Lee Roy Jordan, Randy White, Bill Glass, Jim Myers, Robert Newhouse, John Fitzgerald, John Niland and Timmy Newsome.

A special thanks to Bob Lilly for allowing me to use some of his personal pictures in the book.

And a special thanks to Mike Ditka, for visiting with me regardless of whether he was on the golf coarse or in the middle of doing a commercial.

I know you did so because of your love for Coach Landry and I am grateful.

Last but certainly not least my biggest thanks goes out to my lovely wife Michelle. Michelle had complete confidence in my ability to get this book done. Where others laughed and asked me, "What do you know about writing a book?" Michelle told me it was a great idea and got behind me immediately. Thank you Michelle for never expressing any doubt in me throughout the project although it took a little longer than expected. Thank you for your continual support, for giving me the freedom to spend the time I needed on this project in order to get the book finished. I love you Michelle and I could not have done this without you.

Sincerely,
Michael Thornton

Note to Reader

When I decided to write a book on the Dallas Cowboys the truth is there were a couple initial sizable challenges in front of me. One was the fact that I didn't know any Dallas Cowboys. A second was the fact that I had never written a book. To the first challenge I thought, "Where there is a will there is a way." And to the second challenge I thought, "There is a first time for everything."

Obviously I recognized it would be a long shot to pull this project off but having grown up a Dallas Cowboys fan I learned a valuable lesson about long shots a long time ago from the "Hail Mary." The "Hail Mary" being Roger Staubach's improbable fifty yard touchdown pass to Drew Pearson which lifted the Dallas Cowboys to victory over the Minnesota Vikings with only twenty four seconds left in the 1975 NFC Championship game. The "Hail Mary" taught me this, it doesn't hurt to throw up a prayer and hope for the best.

It doesn't hurt to take a shot downfield. regardless of how improbable a successful outcome may seem, it doesn't hurt to take a shot. If you don't take a shot then you have absolutely no chance at all of being successful. As a guy named Alfred Lord Tennyson once said, "It's better to have tried and failed than to live wondering what would've happened if I had tried."

The last thing I wanted was to have never tried at all. For years I have marveled at the Dallas Cowboys NFL record of twenty consecutive winning seasons and I have wanted to know what was responsible for allowing them to accomplish something no other NFL franchise has been able to accomplish.

I wanted to know what allowed them to be good or great but never bad for two decades? What were the secrets to their success? What were the keys to so many victories? What were the keys to such consistency?

What were the essential principles of their success? What was the foundation of the organization? What was it all built upon? This is what I wanted to know and thankfully, this is what I was able to find out.

In *The Landry Legacy* you will hear from twenty individuals who either played for or were extremely close to legendary coach Tom Landry and in their own words understand what they felt was most responsible for the unmatched stretch of success of the Dallas Cowboys. Individuals such as

Alicia Landry, Roger Staubach, Bob Lilly, Mike Ditka, Dan Reeves, Lee Roy Jordan and others share what they recall being emphasized the most during this historic run.

I believe everyone who picks up the book, Dallas Cowboys fan or not, will greatly appreciate the many valuable life lessons you find in the following pages.

Sincerely,
Michael Thornton

Introduction

When I moved to Dallas in 1969, one of the first people I met was Bill Krisher who was the representative for the local Fellowship of Christian Athletes (FCA) organization.

We became good friends. I had been doing chapels for Bill Glass and the Cleveland Browns and Detroit Lions. Bill Krisher immediately introduced me to Tom Landry and I began doing chapels for the Cowboys.

Coach Landry became one of my best friends. We held a Director's meeting for the Dallas Chapter of FCA once a month at 7 am in his office. It was during those meetings that I noticed his intensive focus. Whether it was being with an FCA group or coaching and leading the Dallas Cowboys, he was focused on the job at hand. I would say this trait was his most important quality.

In addition, Tom was very tough minded. This generally goes hand-in-hand with being a focused individual. He conducted the FCA meetings on a no-nonsense basis. They generally lasted one hour or less and we were on our way by 8 am.

Tom was always committed to his players and to excellence in every area of life. One of the things I noticed right away was that Tom was a goal setter. He not only had goals for the football team, he insisted the players have individual goals as well.

From time to time we would discuss goal setting as it relates to football, family and business. Being involved in the insurance industry, my brother and I were always big on goal setting. We did learn something from Tom that we'd never used before ... you always set two goals – a minimum and a superior. You're committed to making the minimum goal no matter what. The superior is you at your best every day throughout the year and a few breaks along the way.

One year I asked Tom if he would share with me the team goal for the coming season. He said, "The minimum goal is to get to the Super Bowl. The superior goal is to win the Super Bowl." That's how optimistic and precise he was in goal setting. By the way, they won the Super Bowl that year!

The by-product of his coaching was the development of people. Tom always taught his players to prioritize their goals by breaking them down into three major headings – faith, family, and football, in that order.

As you read this book, you will see that Tom had a tremendous impact on his players, both on and off the field. Read and study the principles outlined in this book. They will make you a better person in every area of your life.

In addition, I want to give a special thank you to Michael Thornton for coming up with the idea of this book and for doing the work. He is to be congratulated for taking the time and making the effort to help us remember the principles that Coach Landry taught his family, his teams and his friends.

Garry Kinder

Foreword

One of the things I have learned in life is this; things can change when you least expect it. You never know how something or someone is going to impact your life. For me going to the Dallas Cowboys and playing for Coach Landry dramatically changed my life.

Before I received a call from Coach Landry I really thought I was going to be tending bar somewhere in Pittsburg telling old football stories for the rest of my life. I really did. After spending two dismal years in Philadelphia, where most people didn't even know I played, I really thought my football career was over and I had no idea what I was going to do next.

Then one day to my surprise I got a call from Coach Landry and he said to me, "Mike I don't if you can play anymore or not but we just traded for you so we are going to find out."

Everything changed for me in that moment. One moment I was thinking my football career was over and I didn't know what I was going to do next. The next moment I was presented with the opportunity of a lifetime.

You never know when the opportunity of a lifetime is going to be presented to you. But you have to take advantage of your opportunities.

Coach Landry gave me the opportunity to redeem myself. My time in Philadelphia was not how I wanted my career to end. Coach Landry believed I could still contribute something to his football team and that meant everything to me.

No one in my life impacted me more than Coach Landry did. Certainly my father had great impact on my life. And Coach George Halas had a great impact on my life, but no one has been more instrumental to my success than Coach Landry.

Coach Landry had a system which produced success. His system allowed individuals to get the most out of their individual potential for the sake of accomplishing team goals.

While in Dallas with Coach Landry I became a better player and a better person. Everyone who has either played for him or coached with him, or spent any extended amount of time with him had the opportunity to learn what it took to be successful in life.

Everyone who reads this book will have the opportunity to learn from Coach Landry as well. Coach Landry was a great leader, a great friend and a great example to all of us. Anyone who was close to him was blessed by him.

Sincerely,
Mike Ditka

For The Record

From 1966 to 1985, the Dallas Cowboys never had a losing record. During that time they averaged just over 10 wins and just less than 4 losses for twenty consecutive years. The Dallas Cowboys are the only NFL team to ever compile twenty consecutive winning seasons. Here is a list of how other NFL franchises compare all-time.

Team	Years	Consecutive Winning Seasons
Dallas Cowboys	1966 to 1985	20
Oakland Raiders	1965 to 1980	16
San Francisco 49ers	1983 to 1998	16
Chicago Bears	1930 to 1944	15
Green Bay Packers	1934 to 1947	14
New England Patriots	2001 to 2011	11
New York Giants	1954 to 1963	10
Washington Redskins	1936 to 1945	10
Pittsburgh Steelers	1972 to 1980	9
Kansas City Chiefs	1989 to 1997	9
Indianapolis Colts	2002 to 2010	9

Lee Roy Jordan

#55 Middle Linebacker

Played 14 years for the Dallas Cowboys

Lee Roy Jordan led the University of Alabama to a National Championship in 1961. During his senior season, he recorded 31 tackles in one game, resulting in a 17-0 victory over Oklahoma in the Orange Bowl. When he left Alabama, legendary coach Bear Bryant stated, "He was one of the finest football players the world has ever seen. If runners stayed between the sidelines, he tackled them. He never had a bad day; he was 100 percent every day in practice and in the games."

Drafted by the Cowboys in 1963, Jordan soon earned the nickname "Killer." As team captain for the defense, he ran Coach Landry's "Flex" defense on the field with unmatched intensity. Jordan played for the Cowboys his entire career: from 1963 to 1976.

He led the Cowboys to three Super Bowls, including Super Bowl VI, a convincing 24-3 victory over the Miami Dolphins. He was selected to the Pro Bowl five times, and in 1969 he was named First Team All-Pro.

Twenty five years after retirement, Lee Roy Jordan stands second on the Dallas Cowboys' all-time list for combined tackles. He was first on the list until Cowboys' safety Darren Woodson passed his record in 2004. Jordan is in the Dallas Cowboys Ring of Honor and the College Football Hall of Fame.

Number 01

Develop Your Character

Watch your thoughts, for they become your words,
Watch your words, for they become your actions,
Watch your actions, for they become your habits,
Watch your habits, for they become your character,
Watch your character, for it becomes your destiny.
—*Unknown*

Weakness of attitude becomes weakness of character.
—*Albert Einstein*

I care not what others think of what I do, but I care very much
about what I think of what I do! That is character!
—*Theodore Roosevelt*

Be more concerned with your character than your reputation,
because your character is what you really are, while your
reputation is merely what others think you are.
—*John Wooden*

Everyone tries to define this thing called Character. It's not hard.
Character is doing what's right when nobody's looking.
—*J.C. Watts*

Character, in the long run, is the decisive factor in the life
of an individual and of nations alike.
—*Theodore Roosevelt*

Character

Who you are at the core; that which makes up your core beliefs; your internal makeup; who you are on the inside; your personal traits that define you.

Develop Your Character

Interview with Lee Roy Jordan:

One of the biggest contributors to the success of the Dallas Cowboys was the fact that we had so many high-character guys on our football teams. Coach Landry looked for guys with character, and he found them. Year after year, we were able to find players who were not only physically gifted and talented, but also possessed a great deal of character.

The Cowboys found guys who gave great effort. They found individuals who had a strong work ethic. They found guys who kept their word. If we said we were going to do something, then we did it.

We did not make excuses for ourselves. On the contrary, we were accountable to one another for our actions. We took care of our responsibilities. We did what we were supposed to do, and we did it to the best of our ability.

On a football team and in life, everything begins with character. If character comes first, everything else follows. The Cowboys understood this, and because they did, they developed a great selection process.

Nothing was more important to the Cowboys; not even talent. The Cowboys would take a guy with less talent and more character over a guy with less character and more talent any day of the week; because the guy with more character will out-work, out-hustle, and out-smart the guy with more talent every time.

Individuals with character find a way to win. Individuals without character find a way to lose. Guys with character find a way to overcome. Guys without character make excuses for quitting.

For individuals with high character, quitting is never an option. You persist until you succeed. Failures along the way are just learning experiences. Failures are opportunities to grow in life. They help you become tougher and stronger. They move you closer to accomplishing your goals.

"Something constructive comes from every defeat," Coach Landry used to say. He also said, "Winners never quit trying." As the old saying goes, winners never quit and quitters never win. All of these things were true of the Dallas Cowboys. We never quit working to accomplish our goals.

My most gratifying moment with the Dallas Cowboys was winning our first World Championship over the Miami Dolphins in 1971. Prior to that season, we had been given the nick-name "next year's champion," as we were considered the team that could get close but could not finish. We were considered the team that could get to the big game but could not win it. It was frustrating, but we kept working; we kept finding ways to get better.

We did not allow the criticism to get us down. We allowed it to serve as motivation to work harder. We were relentless in our pursuit of a championship. We had great character. We had a great team. And in 1971, we won it all.

Today, that World Championship ring is on my finger. I am 70 years old, but I still wear that ring. I will always wear my Super Bowl Ring because of what it represents and what it means to me. It represents and reminds me of the character that enabled a group of men to push through adversity and become the best in the world, and I am proud of it.

Throughout my time with the Cowboys, we were very fortunate to have a lot of strong leaders on our teams. We had guys who expected and demanded that things be done a certain way, the right way, and I was one of them. I firmly believed that we had to be accountable to one another. If you said that you were going to do something, then you needed to do it. There was no way around that.

If I was told to do something, then I did it. If they told us to get on a line then I was the first to get on the line; not just sometimes, but every time. You do not lead sometimes, you lead all the time. You do not do things right sometimes, you do things right every time.

That is what it means to have character. Your character does not allow you to do it any other way. Some guys do not always give a hundred percent, and that is a big issue. The issue is a lack of character, and that is an issue that has to be addressed because that will always affect you in a negative way.

Character is the foundation of your life. If your character is not right, then your foundation is not right. If your foundation is not right, then nothing will be right. You have to fix the foundation before you can fix anything else.

Nothing is more important.

None of the teams I was a part of while I was with the Dallas Cowboys ever lacked character. We were not always the most talented team, but we had a lot of guys who accomplished more than their talent should have allowed. We had a lot of overachievers. That is what high-character guys do, they overachieve. Some guys underachieve, other guys overachieve, and the difference is character.

Character compels you to do things a certain way and that was true with the Dallas Cowboys. We did things a certain way. There were certain things that were always true of any of the Dallas Cowboy football teams I was a part of. We always worked as hard as anyone. We never gave up. There was absolutely no "quit" in us. We always believed in ourselves and one another. We always kept fighting until the end. We always found ways to learn from our losses and we always looked for ways to get better, individually and collectively. That is what allowed us to be successful, and I was proud to be a part of it. I was proud to be a part of a great group of men.

Character was our greatest strength. That is how the Cowboys put together twenty consecutive winning seasons, because we did the things that needed to be done in order to be successful year after year. Character is all about having the internal strength to do the difficult things that are required to be successful. Some people are willing to do them, and others are not. Some people have strong character, and others do not.

Character is the willingness to discipline yourself to do the things you need to do that you might not want to do. Becoming successful is not easy. It demands a lot from you; it demands a great deal of discipline. And that's where character comes in.

Character is the willingness to do things the right way all the time. It is the willingness to develop certain right habits. If you start by making a habit of doing things right all the time, then success will follow. If you make a habit of working hard, of never giving up, of always looking for ways to improve, of persisting until you achieve a goal, then success will follow.

That is what we did with the Dallas Cowboys. For us, our success began with finding men with high character, and everything else followed. Character comes first, and success follows.

Lesson Learned

Character, in the long run, is the decisive factor in the life
of an individual and of nations alike.
—*Theodore Roosevelt*

The single most decisive factor in our lives is our character. Our character determines our destiny. My success is dependent upon my character, so developing my character is critical. My character reflects who I am.

As my character grows, I grow. As I develop better habits, I develop better character. The key to developing my character is improving my habits. I need to make a habit of always working as hard as I possibly can. I need to make a habit of always doing the right thing. I need to make a habit of fighting through adversity. I need to make a habit of being relentless and persistent in all my pursuits.

By growing in these areas I develop great character, and great character brings success. Great character lived out does not fail to produce success. Success in life comes as a result of great habits. Great habits are a reflection of great character. My character ultimately determines who I will become and what I will achieve. Developing my character is the key.

Life Exercise

1. Read the quotes at the beginning of the chapter. Reflect on them and then write down the thoughts they bring to your mind.

2. Evaluate your own character. Examine your habits. Ask yourself these questions: How disciplined are you? Do you always do what you say you are going to do? How hard do you work when no one is holding you accountable? Do you take pride in doing things the right way all the time? How often do you do the right thing?

3. Make a decision to do the right thing all the time. Not just when someone is looking. Not just when someone is holding you accountable. Do the right thing all the time. Do what you say you are going to do. Work as hard as you can possibly work. Always give your best effort. Never give less than your best. Take pride in everything you do.

For The Record

Tom Landry currently stands third on the all-time wins list for NFL coaches with 270 wins trailing only George Halas with 324 wins, and Don Shula with 347 wins. Here is how Coach Landry's record of 20 consecutive winning seasons compares to other NFL coaches.

Coaches	Years	Consecutive Winning Seasons
Tom Landry	1966-1985	20
Curly Lambeau	1934-1947	14
Don Shula	1963-1975	13
Marty Schottenheimer	1986-1997	12
Bill Belichick	2001-2011	11
George Halas	1933-1942	10
Tony Dungy	1999-2008	10
Vince Lombardi	1959-1967	9
Chuck Noll	1972-1980	9
Hank Stram	1965-1973	9

George Andrie

#66 Defensive End

Spent 11 years playing for the Dallas Cowboys

George Andrie played his entire professional careerwith the Dallas Cowboys, from 1962 to 1972. Andrie was drafted in the sixth round of the 1962 NFL Draft by the Cowboys as a defensive end, despite not playing his senior season because the sport was dropped at Marquette University.

As a rookie, at 6-6, 250 pounds, Andrie earned a spot in the starting lineup at right defensive end. Andrie had excellent size and strength to hold his ground against the run, yet he had quickness and agility that allowed him to become a great pass rusher. His height also allowed him to excel at batting down passes if he couldn't get to the quarterback. In his first year, he made the NFL All-Rookie team.

Throughout his 11-year career, George Andrie never left the starting lineup with the Dallas Cowboys. He made the Pro Bowl five straight years, from 1965 to 1969. He was named All-Pro in 1969 as well.

Andrie played most of his career next to Hall of Fame defensive tackle Bob Lilly, and together they helped to form the Cowboys' original "Doomsday Defense." He contributed to one of the most dominating defensive Super Bowl performances of all-time in Super Bowl VI. The Cowboys' 24-3 victory over the Miami Dolphins remains the only Super Bowl in which a team has failed to score a touchdown.

Andrie is unofficially credited with a total of 97 sacks, leading the Cowboys in sacks each year from 1964-1967, with a high of 18.5 sacks in 1966. Andrie also had eight straight games with a sack from 1966-1967, achieving the fourth longest such streak in club history. He ranks fifth on the team's all-time sack leaders list. In front of him are Harvey Martin with 113, Randy White with 111, Ed Jones with 105, and DeMarcus Ware with 99.5.

Number 02

Be Completely Committed

Every person who wins in any undertaking must be
willing to cut all resources of retreat. Only by doing so can
one be sure of maintaining that state of mind known as a
burning desire to win - which is essential to success
—*Napoleon Hill*

Desire is the key to motivation, but it is determination and
commitment to an unrelenting pursuit of your goal- a commitment
to excellence- that will enable you to attain the success you seek.
—*Mario Andretti*

The quality of a person's life is in direct proportion to their commitment
to excellence, regardless of their chosen field of endeavor.
—*Vince Lombardi*

Unless commitment is made, there are only
promises and hopes, but no plans.
—*Peter Drucker*

I want to be remembered as the guy who gave his all
whenever he was on the field.
—*Walter Payton*

There are only two options regarding commitment, you are either
in or you are out. There is no such thing as life in-between.
—*Pat Riley*

Commit

To give your word; to give your best; to make up your mind to do something; to see it through, making a dedication to yourself and others. "A commitment made is a debt unpaid."

Be Completely Committed

Interview with George Andrie:

The Dallas Cowboys were completely committed to being one of the best teams in the NFL. The leadership of the organization, Tom Landry and Tex Schramm, was absolutely determined to make that happen. The key to making the Cowboys one of the best teams in the NFL was finding players who were completely committed to being the best they could be. That is what made the Cowboys so good for so long: they found players who were completely sold out to success. Thankfully, I had the opportunity to be one of those players.

After my junior year in college, I did not know if I would ever play football again. The reason why was because in 1960 the University of Marquette disbanded their football program. I was left wondering what I was going to do for my senior year. I could have transferred to a couple of colleges. One was in Oklahoma and the other was in Texas, but I didn't want to move to either state at the time. I could have gone and played in the CFL, but I didn't want to move to Canada either. So I didn't know what I was going to do. I thought my football career might have been over.

Fortunately, Gil Brandt, the scouting director of the Dallas Cowboys, called me and suggested that I stay at Marquette rather than transfer anywhere. He thought I should just focus on getting bigger and stronger. He let me know the Cowboys had an interest in drafting me. He encouraged me to join a private gym and to get a personal trainer, and back then (in 1960) both of those were rare, but that is what I did.

When I realized that I had the opportunity to make the Dallas Cowboys, when the light bulb went off in my head, I made up my mind that I was going to make the most of it. I knew there would be critics. I knew there would be people who would laugh and joke and say, "You are not going to make the NFL. You didn't even play your senior year of college, and now you think you are going to go play in the NFL?" I knew there would be those people, but who cares? I didn't care what other people thought. I was only concerned with what I thought. I thought I could do it, and I was committed to giving myself every opportunity to get it done.

For me, it was a mindset. In my mind, failure was not an option. I was completely committed. I was going to find a way to make the team. To me it was a mental decision, and I believed I could do it. I was going to get in the best shape of my life, and I was not going to let anything get in my way.

Ultimately, I couldn't guarantee success, but I could guarantee myself that I was going to do everything in my power to be successful. If I did not make it, it would not be for a lack of effort. That's the last thing you want in life. You do not want to look back and think, "Well, I could have done more in that situation."

So I gave it everything I had. I got into the best shape of my life. Before that, I had never really lifted weights; in those years it was not really emphasized. But I made it an emphasis, and I ended up getting bigger and stronger. When the draft came around the next year, the Cowboys choose me in the sixth round.

By the time training camp arrived, I was ready to go. I had been waiting for and working toward that day. It was the moment of truth. I remember the first line drill of that training camp: it was an offensive line versus defensive line pass rush drill. I got lined up against a guy the Cowboys thought was going to be a really good offensive tackle for them. On the snap of the ball, I hit the guy as hard I could; I got my arms underneath his pads, and ran right through the guy. I mean, I just picked him up and put him on his back.

Our line coach, Jim Myers, who at the time coached both offensive and defensive line, was a little surprised. I think Coach Myers thought the other guy wasn't ready, so he lined us up again and told the guy, "Hey, this is for real this time. Wake up, let's go." On the snap of the ball, I did the same thing with the same result: hit the guy as hard as I could, got underneath his pads, practically picked him up off the ground, and put him on his back. That happened three or four times with Coach Myers expecting a different result, but there never was. Each time it ended with him on his back.

Now, I have to admit, it was a little surprising, even to me. Honestly, I surprised myself. I mean, I was going against a guy they thought could start at tackle. A part of me thought, "What in the world is going on here?"But another part of me thought, "Well, you have been working out hard." I knew how hard I had been working out, and I knew I was in the best shape of my life. I was strong and I was ready. I had made up my mind that I was going to do it. I was going to make the team. That's what you have to do: you have to make up your mind.

Now it was no cake walk, and I didn't just pick everybody up by their shoulder pads and throw them on their back throughout training camp. But I did make the team, and I started that year(my first year). I started every game. I found a way to get in the starting lineup, and I stayed there from that point on. I ended up playing eleven years with the Cowboys and Coach Landry.

Coach Landry and I got along great. I did the things he wanted done. He and I were on the same page. He expected you to be completely committed to being the best player you could possibly be, and I was.

Coach Landry never got real close to anyone, but he was always available, and he cared about his players. That was good enough for me. He was all business, but football is a business. Coach Landry had a job to do. We all did, and as long as we were all committed to getting our jobs done, then we all got along great.

With the Cowboys, everyone focused on doing their jobs. The Cowboys had an extremely demanding, disciplined system, both offensively and defensively. In order for it to be successful, everyone had to be committed to doing their jobs. On defense, everyone had their specific area of responsibility. We each were to take care of our area, then after that, we would give extra effort and go make a play somewhere else.

We sold out every play. Every man, every play, we sold out. That is why we were so good defensively. We were not just a bunch of individuals running around making plays. We played as a unit and we excelled as a unit. You have to be committed to the team. It does not matter if an individual excels if the team does not. The only thing that matters is the team.

The Dallas Cowboys were one of the first teams to use computers, but a computer cannot measure the size of a man's heart. A computer cannot measure the amount of desire and commitment an individual has for success. The Cowboys did a good job using computers to measure a player's physical talent; but more importantly than that, they did a great job of recognizing players who possessed the intangible qualities a team desperately needs. That is what the Cowboys' success was really tied to: their ability to find guys who were full of heart, desire, and commitment. Those intangibles are a necessity. If those things do not lie within an individual, then he will not be successful.

The Cowboys found winners. Winners are completely committed to winning- no doubt about it. They hate to lose. They refuse to lose. Somehow, someway, they are going to find a way to win.

Winners are going to find a way to overcome any obstacle that attempts to get in their way. They find a way to get their job done. They never give a half-hearted effort. They give everything they have in order to be successful.

In the end, that is all you can do. Give everything you have to give, but when you do, more times than not you will be successful. That is what we found with winning.

The Cowboys had great leadership and commitment from the top, which started with Coach Landry. Coach Landry was the real deal. He was completely committed to the success of the Dallas Cowboys. We each knew that.

Coach Landry was an extremely hard worker and he expected everyone on the team to work as hard as he did. He expected everyone to be as committed as he was, and that is what we were: a team that was completely committed to the success of the Dallas Cowboys. As a team, we didn't take plays off and we didn't take days off. We never just went through the motions. If you are going to do something then you give it all you have to give. We did not leave any amount of effort out.

That is how our team approached everything. There was no acceptance of halfhearted effort at any time. That is how it should be in life: all or nothing. If you are going to do something, then give it your all. If you are not going to give something your all, then don't do it at all; don't even try. If you are going to be successful, then you have to be completely committed to success.

Lesson Learned

"Every person who wins in any undertaking must be willing
to cut all resources of retreat. Only by doing so can one be sure of
maintaining that state of mind known as a burning desire to win -
which is essential to success."
—*Napoleon Hill*

Just as George Andrie so eloquently expressed, "If you are going to be successful then you have to be completely committed to success." I understand success requires an all or nothing commitment from me; either I am in, or I am out. There is no in between, and there is no turning back. If I am not going to be completely committed to it, then why do it? I owe it to myself to be completely committed to my own success.

If I cannot put my whole heart into it, then I have to take myself out of it. A half-hearted commitment leads to a half-hearted effort, and a half-hearted effort never gets the job done. I do not want to look back and wonder if my lack of commitment was the reason why I was not successful. In my pursuit of success, anything less than my best is unacceptable.

A complete commitment to success puts me in the best position to attain success. I recognize that failure is never final unless I quit trying. If I am completely committed to success, then I am determined to never quit trying. Quitting is never an option. Therefore, final failure is never a possible outcome. As Coach Landry said, "something constructive comes from every defeat." Failures along the way are just steps that move me closer to success. I am completely committed to success, and success is the only acceptable outcome.

Life Exercise

1. Read the quotes at the beginning of the chapter. Reflect on them and then write down the thoughts they bring to your mind.

2. Evaluate your own personal level of commitment to success. Ask yourself difficult questions. Are you completely committed to your own success? Are you determined to be successful? Are you willing to do whatever you have to do in order to be successful? Do you consider quitting an option?

3. Make a decision to live your life with an "all in" commitment to anything you do. If you start something, then be completely committed to see it through. Consider the cost from the start. If you start it, then finish it. Never allow quitting as an option.

For The Record

The Dallas Cowboys' 20 Consecutive winning seasons, from 1966-1985, outnumber the total number of winning seasons in the Super Bowl Era (beginning in 1966) for many franchises. The following chart shows 14 examples.

Team	Total Number of Years	Total Number of Winning Seasons
Dallas Cowboys	20 years (1966-1985)	20 Winning Seasons
San Diego Chargers	46 years (1966-2011)	18 Winning Seasons
Cleveland Browns	46 years (1966-2011)	18 Winning Seasons
NY Giants	46 years (1966-2011)	18 Winning Seasons
NY Jets	46 years (1966-2011)	18 Winning Seasons
Chicago Bears	46 years (1966-2011)	17 Winning Seasons
Buffalo Bills	46 years (1966-2011	17 Winning Seasons
Seattle Seahawks	36 years (1976-2011	15 Winning Seasons
Cincinnati Bengals	44 years (1968-2011)	14 Winning Seasons
Detroit Lions	46 years (1966-2011)	13 Winning Seasons
Atlanta Falcons	46 years (1966-2011)	13 Winning Seasons
Oilers/Titans	46 years (1966-2011)	13 Winning Seasons
Arizona Cardinals	46 years (1966-2011)	12 Winning Seasons
Tampa Bay Buccaneers	36 years (1976-2011)	11 Winning Seasons
New Orleans Saints	45 years (1967-2011	11 Winning Seasons

Randy White

#54 Defensive Tackle

Spent 14 years playing for the Dallas Cowboys

During his senior year at the University of Maryland, Randy White won both the Outland Trophy, given to the nation's best interior lineman, and the Lombardi Award, which is annually awarded to college football's best lineman or linebacker.

The Cowboys drafted Randy White in 1975 with the number two overall pick, which they had received from the New York Giants in return for quarterback Craig Morton. The Cowboys initially played White at middle linebacker, intending for him to inherit that position from an aging Lee Roy Jordan.

However, in 1977, Randy's third year, the Cowboys moved him to defensive tackle. The position was a perfect fit for Randy White; he excelled immediately. His success at the position helped the Cowboys win a World Championship that year. Randy was named co-MVPof Super Bowl XII, along with his teammate Harvey Martin.

The 1977 season was the first year Randy White was recognized with both All-Pro and Pro Bowl honors, but it was not the last. For nine consecutive years, from 1977 to 1985, Randy White received both of these awards.

Randy White retired in 1988. He played his entire 14-year career with the Dallas Cowboys. In those 14 years, the Cowboys made the playoffs 10 times, played in 6 NFC Championship games and 3 Super Bowls, and won 2 World Championships.

In 1994, Randy White was inducted into the Pro Football Hall of Fame.

Number 03

Adjust Your Attitude

Nothing can stop the man with the right mental attitude
from achieving his goal; nothing on earth can help the man
with the wrong mental attitude.
—*Thomas Jefferson*

Great effort springs naturally from great attitude.
—*Pat Riley*

Your attitude, not your aptitude, will determine your altitude.
—*ZigZiglar*

Attitude is a little thing that makes a big difference.
—*Winston Churchill*

Excellence is not a skill. It is an attitude.
—*Ralph Marston*

It is our attitude at the beginning of a difficult task which
more than anything else, will affect its successful outcome.
—*William James*

Attitude

Your stance toward; how you feel about something; how you approach things; your perspective, your mindset, your mental makeup.

Adjust Your Attitude

Interview with Randy White:

There was a certain attitude with the Dallas Cowboys that allowed the organization to be so successful. If for some reason, you had a different attitude then theirs, then you had one of two choices. Either you adopted theirs as your own, or you moved on. The attitude was this: you do whatever you have to do, individually and collectively, to get better as a player and as a team, in order to help the organization be successful. Whatever it takes, you do. Whatever they ask you to do, you do. Whatever amount of work that is required, you do. That was the attitude. That was the bottom line. It was that simple.

This was not a problem for me, because that is how I was raised. When I grew up, we worked hard - no questions asked. That was engrained in me by my father. I was expected to work as hard as I possibly could at whatever job I was doing, and I was expected to see things through. If I started something then I was expected to finish it. If I had the wrong attitude toward work, then my father would adjust it for me.

Coach Landry was a lot like my father in that way. Coach expected you to work as hard as you possibly could, and he expected you to find a way to get your job done. That is what he expected. Coach Landry kept pressure on you. He did not let you get comfortable. The expectations never changed. You understood you could be replaced. The team did not revolve around any one person; if you thought it did, then you had better get over yourself, real quick.

It did not matter who you were or how long you had been there. You did not get a pass for anything you had done in the past. You had to work hard to get better every day. Even in the height of my career, when I was considered one of the best in the league at my position, Coach Landry still did not let me get comfortable. He still kept pressure on me. I never took a day off. I never just went through the motions. I understood that I was never going be in the starting lineup just because I was Randy White.

If I was going to continue to be in the starting lineup week after week, year after year, it was going to be because I continued to work harder and perform better than anyone else. Those of us who were considered stars on the team did not get any special treatment. I was there fourteen years and I always thought someone might take my job. My attitude had to be, "I will do whatever I have to do, to be the best I can be, in order to help the team win." That was the required attitude.

As a team, we were always focused. We were always looking for ways to get better. I never thought I had arrived as a player. I never thought I was as good as I could be. There is always room for improvement. In the NFL you always had to look for ways to improve, because it was and is so competitive. There is so much talent. Every team has talent. Talent is not the deciding factor. Attitude is the deciding factor.

You can have all the talent in the world, but if you do not have the right attitude, then you will never live up to the potential of your talent. The right attitude gives you a competitive edge. For the Dallas Cowboys, our competitive edge was tied to our unwillingness to ever get comfortable with where we were. We always believed we could get better, and we were always pushed by the coaches, by other players, and by ourselves, to get better.

The Cowboys had a lot of competitive guys. All of us were always looking for ways to improve. I always started my personal off season workouts two weeks after the end of the previous season. I would give myself a couple of weeks off, and then I would get right back to work. I wanted to get stronger and find other ways to improve my game. I was never satisfied as a player. We were never satisfied as a team. We always remained hungry. Our coaches demanded a lot of us, and we demanded a lot of ourselves. Why? Because we all wanted to be the best that we could be. If that was not your attitude, then you needed to adjust it.

With the Cowboys we were all committed to being the best that we could be. We were all committed to the same things, and the working environment with the Cowboys was tense because we had such high expectations. We had a lot of intense competitors.

If there was a time when you were giving an effort that was less than your best, then you could expect someone to get on you. That is what we all signed up for. Roger Staubach was as intense as they come. Roger worked as hard as anyone. Then there was Lee Roy Jordan. I have never met anyone more intense than he was. If you were not doing what you were supposed to do, and Lee Roy Jordan was around, then you were going to hear about it. If you were not paying attention when you were supposed to be, or you were not giving one hundred percent on the practice field, then he was going to get on you. That is all there was to it.

Coach Landry always had leaders who had the right attitude, and those leaders made sure the right attitude ran through the entire team. That contributed everything to our success. Success requires the right attitude. Winning requires the right attitude: a willingness to do whatever it takes to win. Everybody wants to win, but not everybody has the will to win. Not everyone is willing to pay the price to win.

Hard work is part of winning. You do not win without working hard; it is all a part of the reward. If you have the attitude that you do not like hard work, then you will never be a winner. You need to adjust your attitude, because hard work is required. The Dallas Cowboys had the right attitude toward work and winning, we were willing to do whatever amount of work we had to do in order to win. It was that simple. That was our attitude. That is what we did, and that is why we experienced so much success.

Lesson Learned

"It is our attitude at the beginning of a difficult task which more than anything else, will affect its successful outcome."
—*William James*

Attitude is everything. Until you develop the proper attitude about success, then you will never be successful. The first thing I need to do in my pursuit of success is adjust my attitude accordingly.

My attitude toward success has to be this: whatever it takes to be successful, not only am I willing to do it, but I want to do it. I recognize that success always requires at least four things: hard work, discipline, diligence, and persistence. Any recipe for success includes those four ingredients. They are unavoidable.

If I choose to not work hard, to not be disciplined, to not be diligent and persistent, then I choose not to be successful. If I try to avoid these things, then success will end up avoiding me. So what is my attitude toward hard work, discipline, diligence and persistence? I embrace them and I look forward to them.

Why? Because they are a part of success, and I look forward to being successful. The sooner I adjust my attitude toward these things, the sooner I will be on my way toward success. The choice is mine and I choose success.

Life Exercise

1. Read the quotes at the beginning of the chapter. Reflect on them and then write down the thoughts they bring to your mind.

2. Evaluate your own attitude. Ask yourself these questions: Do others think that you have a good attitude? What is your attitude toward your job? What is your attitude toward these four foundational principles of success: hard work, discipline, diligence and persistence?

3. Make a decision to adjust your attitude as needed. Immediately begin developing a positive attitude toward hard work, discipline, diligence and persistence. Get rid of any negative, lazy attitudes; all they do is hold you back. A negative attitude will not help you accomplish anything. A positive attitude will help you accomplish everything.

For The Record

In the Super Bowl Era, the Dallas Cowboys have more winning seasons than any other team in the NFL, largely due to their twenty consecutive winning seasons from 1966 to 1985. Here are the franchises closest to them in number of winning seasons.

Dallas Cowboys	33
Pittsburgh Steelers	31
Miami Dolphins	29
Minnesota Vikings	27
Oakland Raiders	26
New England Patriots	26
Indianapolis Colts	25
San Francisco 49ers	24
Washington Redskins	24
Denver Broncos	24
Kansas City Chiefs	24
St Louis Rams	24
Green Bay Packers	23

Eddie LeBaron

14 Quarterback

Spent 4 years playing for the Dallas Cowboys

Eddie LeBaron led the University of the Pacific to an undefeated season during his senior year of college. He was the starting quarterback on offense, the starting safety on defense, and the starting punter on special teams.

LeBaron was drafted by the Washington Redskins in 1950. Before joining the Redskins, he served as an officer in the Marine Corps in the Korean War. There he was wounded twice and awarded the Purple Heart and Bronze star.

He played with the Redskins in 1952 and 1953, and then joined the Canadian Football League in 1954. He returned to the NFL in 1955 as the starting quarterback for the Redskins and was named to the Pro Bowl in 1955, 1957 and 1958.

In 1960, the Dallas Cowboys traded a first round pick to the Washington Redskins to obtain LeBaron. LeBaron would be the franchise's first starting quarterback, playing the majority of the time in 1960 and 1961. In 1962, LeBaron split time with his roommate and lifelong friend, Don Meredith. The next season,LeBaron handed the reins to Meredith and served as the Cowboys' backup.

Eddie LeBaron earned his law degree from George Washington University while he played for the Redskins.When he arrived in Dallas, he started practicing law while playing quarterback for the Cowboys.

When he stepped off the football field, he stepped into the broadcast booth. He broadcasted games for CBS and continued practicing law. In 1977, he became the General Manager of the Atlanta Falcons. Under his management, the Falcons went to the playoffs for the first time in franchise history in 1978. They would go to the playoffs three out of the six years he was with the team.

After his time with the Falcons, LeBaron moved back to Northern California where he continued to practice law, started developing land, and started a wine vineyard.

Number 04

Love Your Work

Nothing is work unless you would rather being doing something else.
—*George Halas*

I think I overcame every single one of my personal shortcomings by the sheer passion I brought to my work. If you love your work you will be out there every day trying to do it the best you possibly can and pretty soon everyone around you will catch the passion from you - like a fever.
—*Sam Walton*

The only place success comes before work is in the dictionary.
—*Vince Lombardi*

I can't imagine anything more worthwhile than doing what I most love. And they pay me for it.
—*Edgar Winter*

You never achieve real success unless you like what you are doing.
—*Dale Carnegie*

Love

To be passionate about; to be crazy for; to take great pleasure in; to need, to not want to live without.

Love Your Work

Interview with Eddie LeBaron:

First and foremost, success begins with hard work. You cannot be successful without working hard. You have to get that through your head. There is no way around it. But with that in mind, you ought to take the time to find something you really love doing, because if you love what you do, then you will love the work you have to do in order to be successful at it. You will find the time you invest into your work both rewarding and fulfilling. This was certainly the case for the leadership of the Dallas Cowboys. Tex Schramm, Tom Landry, and Gil Brandt absolutely loved their work. And I believe their love for the game of football played a large role in the success of the Dallas Cowboys.

Tex Schramm, as General Manager, loved running and marketing the team. Gil Brandt, as Player Personal Director, loved searching for and finding talented football players. And Tom Landry, as the Head Coach, loved every aspect of coaching. Finding individuals who loved the game of football was a part of the plan for owner Clint Murchison. And in Tex Schramm, Tom Landry, and Gil Brandt, he found three men who were passionate about the game, who were committed to making Dallas Cowboys successful, and who would stop at nothing until that became a reality.

With those three, Murchison was confidant he had found the right people to lead his organization. Those guys were determined to build a first class franchise, and one of the primary ways they planned on doing that was by finding players who loved the game as much as they did.

Finding guys who loved to play football was a big part of the selection process for the Dallas Cowboys, and I think it was high on their list. They looked for high character guys, they looked for hard workers, and they looked for guys who loved to play the game. This may sound strange, but not every football player is crazy about the game. Some guys are crazy about football, and for others it is just a job. For some, it is simply what they do for a living;

for others football is what they love.

Typically, guys who really love the game of football tend to be high achievers or overachievers. The guys who are not absolutely crazy about the game are more prone to be underachievers. Many times you will see a guy who is a great athlete and he looks like he has all the tools to play in the NFL, and yet, for some reason he never lives up to his potential. The first question I would ask is, "Does he have a love for the game?"

If you do not love the game, then it is harder to get motivated about the amount of work you have to do in order to be successful at it. Now, that was rarely a problem for the Cowboys. The Cowboys found guys who loved to play the game. They found guys who were self-motivated. That is something else I think they looked for.

You rarely have to motivate a guy who loves to play the game of football. When you love the game, then you motivate yourself to be the best football player you possibly can be. You do not want to have to motivate a player every day. Coach Landry certainly didn't. He wanted players who were self-motivated.

That is true with anything you do. If you do not love what you do, then it is harder to get motivated to do it. When you love what you do, you want to do it and you want to be the best you can be at it. That has always been the case for me. I have loved the things I have done in life and I have always wanted to be the best I could be at anything I have done. That was certainly true with football.

I loved playing football, and I thoroughly enjoyed my time in the NFL. In the NFL, I played with the Redskins and the Cowboys. Back then, you played for the love of the game. It was not about the money. They did not pay enough for it to be about the money. You had to have another career in order to really take care of your family back then. I went to law school at George Washington University while I played with the Redskins. I worked my school schedule around my football career. When I came to Dallas, I had two jobs: I was the quarterback for the Cowboys, and I started my law career there as well.

Hard work has always been a part of my life. I was brought up that way. So when I arrived in Dallas in 1960, I fit right in. Coach Landry worked as hard as anyone, harder than most, and he expected you to work hard also. Some people thought Coach Landry expected too much. I didn't think so.

He expected you to be a professional. He expected you to be on time. He expected you to know your assignments. He expected you to be as good as you could be, and he expected you to always look for ways to get better. Anything less than that was unacceptable. Those things were mandatory. Why would anyone expect anything less?

If you are a competitor who loves the game of football, who is passionate about it and committed to it, then those things should come naturally to you. No one should have to force you to do those things. If you have to be forced to do them, then you either do not have much of a work ethic, you are not all that competitive, or you just do not really love the game of football.

When you have people who love what they do, when you have guys who love to play football, then none of these things are a problem. Those things were never a problem with the Cowboys as a whole. Coach Landry's teams were filled with professionals.

The Cowboys had a bunch of guys who loved to play football. They always had a group of guys who loved to compete. They loved to work hard, and they were determined to put themselves in a position to win. Even early on when we struggled as a franchise, it was not because we did not work hard or were not committed. We just did not have the overall talent early on. It takes a while to assemble the talent.

Anyone who knew Coach Landry knew it was only a matter of time before he was successful. Coach Landry was too smart and worked too hard to not eventually be successful. Those were two things you had to respect about Coach Landry: how smart he was, and how hard he worked. I respected everything about him. He was such a competitor. I had played against him through the years, and I knew what an intense competitor he was as a player. He was the same as coach.

He loved the game. He was passionate about it, he was committed to it, and he was determined to be successful at it. That was the type of player Coach Landry looked for. He looked for intense competitors who loved the game, were passionate about it, were committed to it, were determined to be successful at it, and he found them.

In life, it's all about how bad you want something. If you want it bad enough, then you will find a way to get it. It does not matter how much it costs you. This is true of success. Success does not come easily at anything, and it certainly does not come easily in the NFL. But the Dallas Cowboys had a group of men who loved the game of football, and they put their entire heart, mind and soul into being successful at it. Their love for the game compelled them to do whatever was necessary. Ultimately it allowed them to be extremely successful. I appreciated having the opportunity to be a part of it from day one.

Lesson Learned

I can't imagine anything more worthwhile than doing
what I most love. And they pay me for it.
—*Edgar Winter*

Pursuing a career in something you are passionate about creates a path to success. When you love something then you are passionate about it. When you are passionate about it, then you are persistent with it. When you are persistent with it, then it is only a matter of time before you become successful at it.

In order to be successful, I realize that I have to pursue success with a certain relentlessness. Success requires a significant amount of time and hard work. With that in mind, I think Eddie LeBaron is right. I should take the time to find work I love doing. Life is too short to spend all of my time doing something I do not love. Sometimes I have to do what I have to do. But there is still time to find something I love doing.

Why not take the time? I am going to invest my time in something anyway, why not invest it in something I love. Recently, I found the following quote by Sharon Cook and Graciela Sholander. It may seem somewhat idealistic; this passion they define may certainly be hard to find. But ultimately I think it's worth the time it takes to find it.

"If you have ever felt such tremendous enthusiasm and desire for something that you would gladly spend all your waking hours working on it, that you would happily do it without pay, then you have found your passion."

Life Exercise

1. Read the quotes at the beginning of the chapter. Reflect on them and then write down the thoughts they bring to your mind.

2. Evaluate your own passion for what you do. Ask yourself these questions: Do you love your job? Do you enjoy doing what you do? Are you going to be happy doing it the rest of your life?

3. Make a decision to make sure you are doing what you love to do. If you are not doing what you love to do, then do two things. One, figure out what you are passionate about. Two, develop a plan to pursue a career in it.

For The Record

The following is a comparison between the best twenty seasons the Dallas Cowboys had with Coach Landry and their best twenty seasons without Coach Landry, illustrated by number of winning seasons and winning percentage.

Dallas Cowboys	1966 – 1985	Winning Seasons 20
Dallas Cowboys	1966 - 1985	Winning Percentage .705
Dallas Cowboys	1991 – 2010	Winning Seasons 13
Dallas Cowboys	1991 – 2010	Winning Percentage .570

Roger Staubach

#12 Quarterback

Spent 11 years playing for the Dallas Cowboys

Roger Staubach won the Heisman Trophy as a junior in 1963, while leading Navy to a 9-1 regular season record and #2 ranking in the nation. The Midshipmen played in a national championship, but lost to the # 1 ranked team in the country, the University of Texas, in the Cotton Bowl.

Staubach was drafted by the Dallas Cowboys in the 10th round of the 1964 NFL Draft. His pending four-year military commitment to the US Navy kept teams from drafting him earlier.

In 1969, Staubach joined the Dallas Cowboys. For two years, Roger played sporadically while Cowboys veteran quarterback Craig Morton took most of the snaps. When Roger did play, he showed flashes of brilliance.

Staubach took over as the full-time starter of the Dallas Cowboys in the eighth game of the 1971 season, his third year in the league. At the time, the Cowboys were 4-3 and two games behind the Washington Redskins in the race for the NFC East division title.

The Cowboys would not lose another game that year. They won 10 games in a row, culminating in a 24-3 Super Bowl victory over the Miami Dolphins, with Staubach being named the MVP of the game.

Staubach was one of the most exciting NFL players of all time, and certainly of the 1970's. He was known as "Roger the Dodger" for his scrambling ability, "Captain America" as quarterback of America's Team, and "Captain Comeback" for his fourth quarter game-winning heroics. He retired after the 1979 season as the NFL's highest rated passer of all-time, with an 83.4 passing rating.

His eleven-year career consisted of 10 playoff appearances, 7 NFC Championship games, 5 Super Bowls, and 2 World Championships.

Roger played in 6 Pro Bowls, was named to the NFL's 1970's All-Decade Team, and was inducted to the Pro Football Hall of Fame in 1985.

There were eight years in which Roger Staubach was healthy and was the starting quarterback for the majority of the games. In those 8 years, he led the Cowboys to the playoffs every year, made it to the NFC Championship Game 6 times, made it to the Super Bowl 4 times, and won the Super Bowl twice. This is a record he is proud of and fairly content with.

Number 05

Build A Team

Alone we can do so little; together we can do so much.
—Helen Keller

Individual commitment to a group effort - that is what makes a team work, a company work, a society work, a civilization work.
—Vince Lombardi

I am a member of a team, and I rely on the team, I defer to it and sacrifice for it, because the team, not the individual, is the ultimate champion.
—Mia Hamm

The nice thing about teamwork is that you always have others on your side.
—Margaret Carty

Great teamwork is the only way we create
the breakthroughs that define our careers.
—Pat Riley

The main ingredient in stardom is the rest of the team.
—John Wooden

Team

A group organized together, pulling together, joining together for collective pursuits, focused on a common goal, working together to successfully accomplish specific tasks.

Build a Team

Interview with Roger Staubach:

Building the right team of people is the key to success for any organization. If you are unable to put together the right team of people in the right places, then you will never experience any real measure of success. Individuals have to be able to work together as a cohesive unit. The leadership of the Dallas Cowboys understood these things as well as anyone, and their ability to consistently put together a great team of people allowed them to be extremely successful.

It all started with the owner. Owner Clint Murchison found the right people and placed them in key positions of leadership. He began by hiring Tex Schramm to be the General Manager. Then they hired Tom Landry as Head Coach, and then they brought in Gil Brandt as the Personnel Director.

Those three men made a great team. The three of them built the Dallas Cowboys. They worked well together and they recognized that. Each of them had their own areas of responsibility, and they each let the other do their job. They trusted one another. There was great chemistry between the three of them.

There was also great chemistry on the football team. Coach Landry made sure of that. He was always very mindful of the need to put together a group of individuals who could work together. He knew the key to winning was the ability to stay focused on the objective, so the team needed to be made up of a group of people who could help one another stay focused on the collective objective.

You have to find individuals who can stay focused and avoid individuals who can become a distraction. You have to avoid distractions. That is the challenge. Distractions will derail a team.

Under Tom Landry, the Dallas Cowboys were always focused. We were always focused on our goals, our objectives, and our preparation. We set goals at the beginning of the year. We established objectives that would allow us to accomplish our goals, and then we set out to accomplish our objectives through thorough preparation. That was our system, and everyone on the team had to buy into it.

Everyone on the team had to participate in the process. Everyone had to be willing to work hard in the area of preparation in order to accomplish our goals and objectives. Regardless of how talented you were, you still had to prepare as thoroughly as possible.

Coach Landry expected everyone to do their job, and in order to do your job, you had to know your assignments. We had a complex system, so if you were going to know your assignments, if you were going to be thoroughly prepared to play, then you were going to have to put in a lot of hard work.

That is where it begins. You have to find guys who will work hard. Before you add anyone to your team, you ought to find out how hard the individual is willing to work. On a team, you are dependent upon one another. You can have ten guys who know their assignments, and ten guys who do their jobs, but if the eleventh guy does not know his assignment and does not do his job then you are in trouble.

On a team, your personal success is dependent upon other individuals. That is why you have to have people you can trust. If you cannot trust someone, then they do not need to be on your team. Coach Landry understood that, and he looked for guys he could trust.

Coach Landry looked for great competitors who had great character. That is the type of player he wanted on his team. He found that to be the winning combination of attributes. Great competitors with great character were the type of guys he could trust.

Those types of guys can be counted on. You can count on them to work as hard as they can in their pursuit of success. Competitors with character are always going to give you maximum effort. They are always going to give everything they have to give in order to win.

When I joined the Cowboys in 1969, they already had a team full of competitors who had great character, and they were having success. They were winning and making the playoffs when I got there. They had guys like Bob Lilly, Lee Roy Jordan, Chuck Howley, Dan Reeves, and Don Meredith, just to name a few, and all of those guys were great competitors who worked as hard as anyone.

The Cowboys had already begun to build a winning environment. That's what good teams do - they build an environment or a culture of success. A good team creates an expectation of success. They expect to be successful because they know as a team they are doing the right things. That was happening with the Cowboys when I arrived.

The Cowboys had great leadership and great chemistry. They had a group of guys who fit well together and worked well together, which you cannot underestimate. You have to have guys who can get along. You cannot afford to have too many clashing personalities or egos on a team. Usually guys who like to win find a way to get along.

Winners are more interested in the team and winning than anything else. Winners find a way to put other things aside and focus on accomplishing team goals. The guys who are more interested in themselves and their individual goals can ruin everything for everyone else. The Cowboys had too many strong leaders to allow that to happen. If a particular player was creating an issue on the team, then either Coach Landry or one of the leaders on the team would deal with it.

Honestly, that was rarely a problem for the Cowboys. All and all, they had a great deal of success finding team guys. Again, Coach Landry knew the type of player he wanted. He knew the type of players he needed.

Coach Landry was not a real emotional guy, but he put emotional leaders on the field in key positions, and he would communicate with those of us who were leaders. Then he would let us lead. He would let us deal with a lot of problems. That was a part of our role and responsibility. Coach Landry prepared the team, but he allowed and expected the captains of the team and the leaders of the team to handle certain things on and off the field.

Watching how Coach Landry handled all of these situations taught me a number of valuable lessons which I carried with me into my business life. Things I learned on the field, I used off the field. Success in any team sport creates a great analogy for what it takes to be successful in business and in life in general, for that matter.

In business and in life, you have to get the right people around you. You have to find hard workers. You have to have strong leaders. Everyone has a role and a responsibility. Everyone on the team has to be able to trust one another. You have to get rid of and avoid those who are only interested in themselves and those who just want to take and not give. You need givers not takers.

You have to find those who are interested in the overall success of the group. You have to build the right chemistry. You have to find those who can work together and have success as a team. You have to find those who are willing to set common goals and are willing to do whatever is necessary to achieve them.

As I built my own business, I implemented the team principles I learned while I was with the Cowboys. As I did, I began to understand these things on a whole new level. You quickly realize how important others are to your success. You quickly realize that you cannot do everything yourself. You need help. You need the help of a team. And the more successful you become, the more dependent you become upon the team. You have to have people around you who you can trust and count on.

A team of people you can trust and count on can get you places you could not get on your own. Life is not just going to give you anything. It takes hard work. As my friend Garry Kinder says, "It takes a lot of unspectacular work in order to get spectacular results." The challenge is to find others who are willing to work hard with you.

Things are not always going to go well. There are times when we are going to fail; it is a part of life. You have to find a group of people who will persevere through the difficult times, because difficult times are going to come. You have to find those who will fight with you through adversity. Adversity will come, and adversity reveals true character.

Adversity also reveals real competitors. I had the opportunity to play on a number of teams full of competitors with great character while I was with the Cowboys, but probably the most memorable of those teams was the 1971 team.

That year, we were very inconsistent through the first half of the season. We lost to the Chicago Bears and that put us at 4-3 for the year through the first seven games. We were struggling, and it was difficult because we had such high hopes for the season.

We had high expectations for that football team, and we were in jeopardy of letting the season get away from us. It looked like we might not even come close to achieving our goals. But in that moment, halfway through the season, Coach Landry got with the team leaders and reminded us of what we needed to do to be successful.

We went out to practice that next week and we rallied together as a team. We reminded one another of what we were committed to. We got our priorities straightened out. We helped each other get focused on our responsibilities. We went back to work, and our team went on to win the next ten games in a row, culminating with a win over the Miami Dolphins in the Super Bowl VI. Our team fought through the early adversity and ended up winning a championship.

That was a special year. I learned a lot from that 1971 Championship team. Most of all, I learned that if you have the right people, in the right place, focused on the right priorities, then miracles can happen. A team of competitors with character, thoroughly prepared and diligently focused, can overcome any obstacle and accomplish any desired objective. I learned from my time with the Dallas Cowboys that the key to success is building the right team of people.

Lesson Learned

The main ingredient in stardom is the rest of the team.
—*John Wooden*

One of the main ingredients of our personal success is the team of people we surround ourselves with. In life we need to stay focused on our goals and objectives. Therefore, we need to surround ourselves with people who challenge us, who encourage us, who motivate us, and who help us to stay focused on the things we are pursuing in life.

We need people who remind us of who we are and remind us of what we are going after. We don't need people who help us compromise. We need people who will help us stay committed. We need individuals who are interested in our success. And we, in turn, are interested in their success.

The people I surround myself with in life make up my own team, and I do not need people around me who distract me. Life already has enough distractions. I need people who help me stay focused. There are already enough obstacles in life. I need people around me who help me overcome those obstacles. I need to surround myself with high character individuals. One of the main ingredients to my success is putting a team of people around me who will help me become successful.

Life Exercise

1. Read the quotes at the beginning of the chapter. Reflect on them and then write down the thoughts they bring to your mind.

2. Evaluate the type of people you have around you right now. Ask yourself these questions: Do they challenge you, encourage you, and motivate you? Do they help you stay focused, or do they distract you? Do they push you forward or pull you back? Are they high character individuals? Are they successful in their own right?

3. Make a decision to find and surround yourself with the type of people who are interested in your success. People who will help you stay focused. High character individuals who help you overcome obstacles. Those who will help you continue moving forward, toward your goals. Those who will help you become successful.

For The Record

Tom Landry and the Dallas Cowboys compiled 13 Division Titles within a twenty year span. Between 1966 and 1985, the Dallas Cowboys finished in first place 13 out of 20 seasons. Coach Landry is the only NFL coach to win 13 Division Titles within a twenty year period. Here is a list of how other NFL coaches stack up.

Coaches	Years	Division Titles
Tom Landry	1966-1985	13
Don Shula	1971-1990	10
Chuck Noll	1972-1991	9
George Halas	1932-1951	9
Paul Brown	1950-1969	9
Curly Lambeau	1929-1948	8
Marty Schottenheimer	1985-2004	7
Chuck Knox	1973-1992	7
Dan Reeves	1984-2003	6
Bill Parcells	1984-2003	5

Robert Newhouse

#44 Running Back

Spent 12 years playing for the Dallas Cowboys

Robert Newhouse was a great college running back, and one of the greatest to ever play at the University of Houston. Newhouse broke many school records, some of which still stand today, such as the single season rushing record of 1757 yards set back in 1971. Newhouse also has 16 games where he rushed for over 100 yards and 4 games where he rushed for over 200 yards.

After his remarkable college career, he was a second round draft pick of the Dallas Cowboys in the 1972 NFL Draft. Having grown up in Texas, Newhouse hoped to play professional football somewhere outside the state; but Dallas was his new home.

Newhouse averaged 4.1 yards per carry over the course of his career. In 1975, he led the team in rushing with 930 yards. He was the team's second leading rusher in 1974, 1976, 1977, 1978, 1979, and 1980, where he averaged over 500 yards a season.

There are only four players in front of Newhouse on the Dallas Cowboys' all-time rushing list. Emmitt Smith is number one, Tony Dorsett is number two, Don Perkins is number three and Calvin Hill is number four. Newhouse stands in front of guys like Marion Barber, Hershel Walker, Walt Garrison, and Julius Jones.

Newhouse played fullback, but could be used as a primary running back. He was not tall, but he was big strong. He was built very low to the ground and had tremendous leg strength. Newhouse thrived on second effort, picking up the nicknames "The House" and "The Human Bowling Ball."

The Cowboys made the playoffs 11 out of the 12 years that Newhouse played with the team. They played in 8 Conference Championship Games, 3 Super Bowls and they won 2 World Championships.

Number 06

Learn To Listen

Courage is what it takes to stand up and speak; courage
is also what it takes to sit down and listen.
—*Winston Churchill*

When people talk, listen completely. I like to listen. I have learned a great
deal from listening carefully. Most people never listen.
—*Ernest Hemingway*

No man ever listened himself out of a job.
—*Calvin Coolidge*

I remind myself every morning: Nothing I say this day will teach me
anything. So if I'm going to learn, I must do it by listening.
—*Larry King*

You learn when you listen. You earn when you listen –
not just money but respect.
—*Harvey Mackay*

Most of the successful people I've known are the ones
who do more *listening than talking.*
—*Bernard M. Baruch*

Listen

To give one's attention to; to focus on; to hear what is being communicated; the act of hearing and retaining information.

Learn To Listen

Interview with Robert Newhouse:

The Dallas Cowboys were successful as a team because we learned to listen to our leadership. As players, first and foremost we learned to listen to Tom Landry. We listened to what he said. We did what he said, and we had success because of it.

This was true of our team and it was certainly true with me personally. The fact is, I did not have success with the Dallas Cowboys until I finally realized I needed to learn to listen. Coach kept telling me to listen, but it took me a little while to do it.

Why it took me so long, I don't know; probably because up until that point I had been able to figure things out on my own. You know, prior to joining the Cowboys, for the most part I had been able to rely upon my natural ability. I was able to have success on the football field because of my natural ability.

With football, I realized at a young age that if I put my mind to it, then I could do it. Now, that was not true of all sports. Football was the only sport that was true of. I could not shoot the ball well enough to succeed in basketball. I could not run fast enough to succeed in track. But with football, I knew that if I put my mind to it, then I could be successful at it.

My natural ability provided me with the opportunity to be successful in football. My natural ability allowed me to move up from one level of competition to another, with each level presenting new challenges. But thankfully, I was able to overcome until I found myself in the NFL, playing with the Dallas Cowboys.

As soon as I got onto the practice field with the Cowboys, I understood that the NFL was a whole different world. At that point, I understood that natural ability only gets you so far in life, and I quickly recognized that I still had a lot to learn if I was going to be successful in the NFL.

Initially, I simply refused to listen. I was so hard-headed and stubborn. You couldn't tell me anything. I thought I knew everything, and if I didn't know something, then I thought I could figure it out on my own. I thought I could find a way to make it work myself. I didn't need anybody to help me. At least that is what I thought; but that type of thinking did not work with Tom Landry and his system

With the Cowboys' system, everything was dependent upon you trusting Tom Landry, and initially, I didn't know if I could trust Coach Landry. I had this battle going on in my mind between trying to figure things out on my own versus learning to listen to what Coach Landry was telling me. It took me a little while to realize I could trust him. That is the truth. I could have saved myself a whole lot of frustration and got myself on the football field a whole lot sooner if I would have learned to listen a whole lot faster.

Thankfully, one day I had a conversation with another player who really helped me with this. It was Walt Garrison.He probably does not know this (I never discussed it with him), but he impacted me and my career like no one else.

Here is what happened. When I got to the Cowboys, Walt Garrison played in front of me, and he stayed in front of me for a couple of years. Not only did he play in front of me, but they actually gave Walt the ball quite a bit.

That really puzzled me, because I looked at this guy, and I knew that I was a better athlete than he was. I was bigger than he was. I was stronger than he was. I was faster than he was. I could jump higher than he could. Physically there was nothing that I could not do better than him. That was just a fact.

So how was it that he was in the starting lineup and I was watching from the sideline? I was perplexed. I did not understand how this little white guy stayed in front of me, and I would have never said it publicly, but I did wonder at times if it was a race thing.

So one day, I had to ask Walt. I went up to Walt Garrison and confronted him with this. I said, "Walt, you know that I am a better athlete than you are. You know that I am bigger, I am stronger, I am faster, and I am an all-round better athlete than you are, so how is it that you continue to play, and I continue to stay on the sidelines?"

He looked at me and he said, "Well I won't argue with you Robert, everything you said is true. But here is something else that is true. You do not know the plays as well as I do. You do not know the audible's as well as I do.

You do not know the opposing defenses as well as I do. You do not know what Coach Landry wants and expects as well as I do. But other than that, you are right; you are better than me.

Then Walt went on about his business. He probably never thought another thing about it, but I was left there thinking about how right he was. That conversation was a wakeup call for me, and that moment served as a turningpoint in my career.

Those words by Walt Garrison stopped me in my tracks because I knew that what he said was true. He was right; I did not know the plays, the audibles, the opposing defenses, and the expectations of Coach Landry as well as I needed to.

Why did I not know all those things? Because I had not been listening. I had been trying to figure things out on my own. I was trying to lean on my own natural physical ability, rather than simply listen to the Coach. When I began listening, I began learning. When I began learning, I began playing.

Seriously; when I started listening, I started playing. At first I was so naïve. I didn't understand how much I didn't know about the game of football. And the reality was that Coach Landry had the game of football figured out. He was an authority on the game of football. I just needed to trust his authority.

Coach Landry knew where everybody was and where everyone was going to be on a football field. If he said there was going to be a hole in a specific spot, then nine times out of ten there was a hole in that specific spot. If you learned to listen to him and do what he told you to do, then you would be successful.

When I learned to listen, the game became easy. Once I directed my focus to the mental side of the game it became easy. In the NFL, you have to be as mentally strong as you are physically strong. The mental side of the game is just as important, or even more important, than the physical side.

Coach Landry's system was complex, but he would make your role and your responsibilities clear, if you would listen. They would show you what to do on the field and in meetings, if you would listen. Coach Landry always made sure we were thoroughly prepared.

He understood the key to winning was having a good game plan. The key to winning with a good game play is execution. The key to execution is preparation, and the key to preparation is first and foremost, listening, and listening well.

We had plenty of guys come through the organization who did not learn this lesson quickly enough. Because the reality was, if you did not learn to listen then it was only a matter of time before you were let go by the team. Personally, I was lucky they kept me around as long as they did.

Some guys were not so fortunate. I remember one guy in particular, a guy by the name of George Peoples. George had all kinds of talent. He was 6'0", 215 pounds, and the guy could run. I thought he had the potential to be a really good player for the Cowboys. But as I watched him,I realized he was not picking up certain things because he was not listening to the coaches. He was trying to do things on his own, and I knew the coaches were getting frustrated with him.

So I thought I could offer him some advice, since I had been through the same situation. But when I went to him to talk to him, he didn't want anything to do with it. It went in one ear and out the other. He just told me, "Hey, I got this." A couple of weeks later, George Peoples was gone. He didn't listen to me or anyone else, and the team let him go. I hated that; it was a shame.

He went on to play with a couple of other teams, but he did not have the type of success I thought he could have had. He had so much natural ability. But that is the case with so many people. There are all kinds of people who do not live up to their potential because they will not learn to listen.

If you are going to have success with an organization, then you have to learn to listen. You have to learn to trust those who are leading the organization. You have to listen to what they say, and do what they say. That is why the Dallas Cowboys had so much success as an organization.

We trusted our leadership. We listened to what they said, and we did what they said. Because of it, we were extremely well-prepared and ready to play each week. We were all on the same page, and that allowed us to be successful.

That's how a football team puts itself in a position to be successful, by paying attention and listening to leadership. That's how I put myself in a position to be successful. I finally paid attention and listened. That's how it works for any of us in anything we do. Listening is a key component of success. The Cowboys listened to Coach Landry and we won a lot because of it.

Lesson Learned

You learn when you listen. You earn when you listen –
not just money but respect.
—*Harvey Mackay*

Learning to listen is an invaluable lesson, and learning to listen well is an invaluable skill. Even though you may be one of those people who have an uncanny ability to figure things out on your own, at some point in time everyone has to learn to listen. Ultimately there are only two things that would keep you from learning to listen: either pride or laziness.

In my pursuit of success, neither pride nor laziness will stand in my way. I would be a fool to allow that to happen. Listening and learning are both a part of the process of becoming successful. I will not become successful if I do not learn to listen.

If I do not learn to listen, then I cheat myself. Successful people know what it takes to be successful. The quickest way for me to learn is to give others my undivided attention, to watch, and to listen. If I cannot do that, then I will never be successful. For me, my plan is to listen to others who have been successful, and apply the same principles of success to my own life.

Life Exercise

1. Read the quotes at the beginning of the chapter. Reflect on them and then write down the thoughts they bring to your mind.

2. Evaluate what type of listener you are. Ask yourself these questions: Are you a willing listener? Do you readily or reluctantly listen to others? Do you give others your undivided attention? Do you listen to the expertise of others, or do you try to figure everything out on your own?

3. Make a decision to improve your listening skills. Do not let pride, stubbornness, or laziness get in the way of you listening. Give others your undivided attention. Seek out others who have been successful and listen to what they have to say. Learn from the expertise of others.

For The Record

The 13 Division Titles the Dallas Cowboys won in twenty years under Tom Landry matches the total number of Division Titles the Washington Redskins have won in the history of their franchise. Six of the Redskins titles were captured before 1950. There are 12 teams who have been in the NFL for at least 30 years who have not won a total 13 Division Titles in the entire history of their organization.

Team	Years in the League	Number of Division Titles
Washington Redskins	80 years	13 Division Titles
Philadelphia Eagles	79 years	12 Division Titles
Denver Broncos	52 years	11 Division Titles
Buffalo Bills	52 years	10 Division Titles
Oilers-Titans	52 years	9 Division Titles
Detroit Lions	82 years	8 Division Titles
Kansas City	52 years	7 Division Titles
Cincinnati Bengals	44 years	7 Division Titles
Seattle Seahawks	36 years	7 Division Titles
Tampa Bay Buccaneers	36 years	6 Division Titles
New Orleans Saints	45 years	5 Division Titles
Atlanta Falcons	46 years	4 Division Titles
New York Jets	52 years	4 Division Titles

Garry Kinder

Kinder Brothers International

Enjoyed 40 years of friendship with Tom Landry

Garry Kinder had the privilege of being one of Tom Landry's closest friends. For years, Garry met with Coach Landry on a weekly basis. Garry and his brother Jack implemented Coach Landry's goal-setting system and taught it to countless others across the country. Many of the Kinder Brothers' success principles were learned by watching Tom Landry lead the Dallas Cowboys.

As Co-CEO of The KBI Group, Garry Kinder is a sales and management consultant to more than 300 companies spread throughout the world. His experience in life insurance began at age 20, when he began selling for The Equitable while a junior in college. He graduated from Illinois Wesleyan University. Garry became the youngest agent in Illinois to achieve membership in the Million Dollar Round Table. After spending five years as an agent, he became a Field Manager in Bloomington, Illinois; Akron, Ohio; and Detroit, Michigan. He was eventually named Regional Vice President for The Equitable in Dallas.

Today, he still maintains an agent's license with the Equitable. He and his brother, Jack, qualified for the 2001 & 2003 Million Dollar Round Table. Marshall Wolper, a past President of the Round Table, has said, "The Kinder Brothers are masters in the presentation and strategy of selling. They have taught their procedures and techniques to thousands and indirectly to tens of thousands."

The Kinders directed the popular Purdue Institute for 35 years. They have also produced over 40 resource tools, including CDs, videos, and software packages that continue to assist Financial Professionals and Field Management. In addition, they have authored eight best-selling books, including Winning Strategies in Selling, written with Roger Staubach. Their book, Building the Master Agency, is a best seller in the financial services industry. Roger Staubach describes Garry Kinder as one of the finest individuals he has ever met.

Number 07

Set Some Goals

If you want to be happy, set a goal that commands your thoughts, liberates
your energy, and inspires your hopes
—*Andrew Carnegie*

Without goals and plans to reach them, you are like a ship that has set sail
with no destination
—*Fitzhugh Dodson*

A goal without a plan is just a wish.
—*Larry Elder*

Goals are dreams with deadlines.
—*Diana Scharf Hunt*

First, have a definite, clear practical ideal; a goal, an objective. Second, have
the necessary means to achieve your ends; wisdom, money, materials, and
methods. Third, adjust all your means to that end.
—*Aristotle*

It must be borne in mind that the tragedy of life does not lie in not reaching
your goal. The tragedy of life lies in having no goal to reach.
—*Benjamin E Mays*

You are never too old to set another goal or dream a new dream
—*C.S. Lewis*

Set your goals high and do not stop until you get there.
—*Bo Jackson*

Goal

A focus point for the mind, a target for the mind to aim for, that which motivates both the mind and the body producing energy for accomplishment.

Set Some Goals

Interview with Garry Kinder:

Coach Landry was all about setting goals. There was no greater contributor to the success of the Dallas Cowboys than their ability as an organization to set goals. After setting a goal, they would develop a plan to accomplish those goals. Then, they would implement a means of evaluating how effectively they were moving toward their goals. They would make needed adjustments according to their evaluations. The Cowboys had these things down to a science, and it began with setting some goals.

The Dallas Cowboys had two sets of goals. They had both team goals and individual goals. For each area and each player, there was both a minimum goal and a superior goal. Coach Landry's philosophy was that there should be both a goal that was well within reach (a reasonable goal) and a goal that would be difficult to reach (an outstanding goal). Both needed to be in place, and a plan needed to be developed to accomplish both. Throughout the year they would consistently evaluate and measure how effectively they were moving toward attaining those goals.

For example, offensively they may have had two goals for their average rushing yards per carry. Their minimum goal may have been to average 4 yards per carry, and their superior goal may have been to average 4.8 yards per carry. One year, their minimum team goal was to make it to the Super Bowl and their superior team goal was to win the Super Bowl. That is when they were loaded with talent, and Coach Landry had high expectations of his team. Those are the type of goals they set.

Anyone who was close to Coach Landry saw how effective these methods were and began using them in some capacity. My brother, Jack, and I adopted these goal-setting procedures at Kinder Brothers Associates. We both applied them to our own lives and shared them with those we came in contact with.

When we trained people within our business and in conferences all over the world, we taught them Tom Landry's goal setting system.

Coach Landry understood that without goals, neither teams nor individuals would ever reach their full potential. He recognized the mind of man to be a goal-achieving instrument. We are made to be goal-achievers, and goals are set to be met. There is an expectation. Napoleon Hill said, "What the mind of man can conceive and believe, the mind of man can achieve." My brother and I added to the end of that statement, "with the blessing of God." What the mind of man can conceive and believe the mind of man can achieve, with the blessing of God.

If you do not have a goal, then your mind will go wherever. Your mind will wander aimlessly. You have to feed the mind goals. Earl Nightingale was the first to really push this understanding. In the 50's Nightingale said, "We become what we think about," and he believed that was the difference between those who were and were not successful.

Nightingales' reasoning went like this: if we become what we think about, then if we set our minds on certain worthwhile goals, we will attain those goals. Goals are essential. If there are no goals, then there is no real direction. Goals set the course for the mind and the body. You have to give your mind and body goals.

You have to have goals in every walk of life, personally, in business, and in your family. Of course, I implemented goals in my personal life and in my business life; but I also implemented goals in my family life. I implemented this system in my own home.

For years, our family has sat down together and set goals for ourselves. Every year, we plan family goals. We discuss what we can do better as a family. It is something my daughters started doing at a young age, and now they have passed it onto their own kids. My grandchildren have implemented Coach Landry's goal setting system. It is invaluable.

For Coach Landry goal setting was another part of preparation, and he was all about preparation. Not being prepared was unacceptable. Not setting goals is the same as not being prepared. As they say, "No one plans to fail, they simply fail to plan." Coach Landry never failed to plan, and never failed to set goals.

He always kept goals in his mind and in the minds of the players. They were written down. They were understood. They were measured. They were on the walls of the locker room. You have to remind your mind of where you are going. You have to remind yourself why you are doing what you are doing. Direct your mind, and the body will follow. The body and the mind will go for goals every time, if you have them.

One of the worst things you can do in life is to not set goals. If you do not want to be successful then do not set goals. Success without goals is called a fluke. Successful people set goals. Really successful people set really good goals. Coach Landry was really good at setting goals. And nothing contributed more to the success of the Dallas Cowboys then their thorough system of goal setting.

Lesson Learned

Without goals and plans to reach them, you are like
a ship that has set sail with no destination
—Fitzhugh Dodson

Nothing is more important in the pursuit of success than setting goals. Your goals establish a strategy for how you are going to become successful, and they empower you to fulfill it. Goals develop objectives for the mind and the body and provide the energy for diligent, disciplined effort.

Ultimately, goals are my best friend. Goals help me accomplish what I want to accomplish in life. They have the ability to move me in the direction I desire to go. Goals motivate me to take action. Goals are the foundation of my plan. I have to have a plan for success, and my plan is built around my goals.

My goals remind me what I want in life. They are what I am going after. My mind goes after goals. Goals are a part of my mind's internal GPS system. I place the goal in my mind, and my mind heads in that direction. If I do not place the goal in my mind, then my mind has no particular direction to go. Goals are an essential part of success. I have my goals, my goals are written down, and my goals are moving me toward success.

Life Exercise

1. Read the quotes at the beginning of the chapter. Reflect on them and then write down the thoughts they bring to your mind.

2. Evaluate your goals. Ask yourself these questions: Do you have goals? Are they written down? Are they clear? Do you have a plan for accomplishing them? Do you have both reasonable goals, and outstanding goals? Are your goals moving you to action?

3. Make a decision to improve your goal setting skills. If you haven't already, immediately take the time to set some goals. Set some goals that are both well within your reach and goals that are well outside of your reach. Allow your goals to stretch you. Make the goals clear. Have them written down. Have a plan to accomplish them. Evaluate your progress. Have someone hold you accountable.

For The Record

In the Super Bowl Era (beginning in 1966), the Dallas Cowboys have captured 21 Divisional Titles, three times as many as the Washington Redskins with 7. Here is how they stack up against all of their NFC East foes.

Dallas Cowboys	21
New York Giants	8
Philadelphia Eagles	8
Washington Redskins	7

Bob Lilly

#74 Defensive Tackle

Spent 14 years playing with the Dallas Cowboys

Bob Lilly was an All-American while playing defensive tackle at Texas Christian University. Lilly was a first-round draft pick of the Dallas Cowboys in the 1961 NFL Draft. He was the first draft pick of the franchise.

Tom Landry built his "Doomsday Defense" around Bob Lilly. With a combination of size, strength, and quickness, Lilly dominated consistently. Initially, he played defensive end but was moved to defensive tackle. As a tackle, Lilly was a first-team All-NFL choice every year from 1964 through 1969, then again in 1971.

Bob Lilly was known as "Mr. Cowboy." He was the heart and soul of the Cowboys, helping them move from being one of the worst NFL teams in the league to one of the best, leading the team to two Super Bowls and an NFL Championship over the Miami Dolphins in 1971.

He is a member of the College Football Hall of Fame and the NFL Hall of Fame. He is unquestionably one of the greatest football players to ever play the game. He revolutionized the defensive tackle position in the NFL.

Lilly was the first member of the Dallas Cowboys Ring of Honor and is still recognized by many as the greatest Dallas Cowboy of all-time.

Number 08

Develop A Plan

It takes as much energy to wish as it does to plan.
—*Eleanor Roosevelt*

Put your plan in writing. The moment you complete this, you will have definitely given concrete form to the intangible wish.
—*Napoleon Hill*

Our goals can only be reached through a vehicle of a plan, in which we must fervently believe, and upon which we must vigorously act. There is no other route to success.
—*Stephen A. Brennan*

Plan your work for today and every day, then work your plan.
—*Margaret Thatcher*

You were born to win, but to be a winner, you must plan to win, prepare to win, and expect to win.
—*ZigZiglar*

Plan your work and work your plan.
—*Vince Lombardi*

Plan

A list of steps, a step by step description of intended actions which creates a strategic road map precisely detailing how one will move from point a to point b in order to reach specific designated goals.

Develop A Plan

Interview with Bob Lilly:

In life, success begins with a plan. You do not become successful without a plan. Success does not happen by accident. The same is true in football. You do not win by accident. You do not win football games without a plan. You win as a result of executing a well-developed plan. That is why the Dallas Cowboys won so many games. Because Coach Landry always provided us with a well-developed game plan, and he always prepared us well to execute the plan.

Nothing affects the outcome of a game more than the game plan. Talent is not the deciding factor in the outcome. Every team in the NFL has talent. Yes, some teams have more talent than others, but whether you win or lose is not determined by talent alone.

Many times, a team with less talent will win, and a team with more talent will lose. Why? Because ultimately, winning comes down to how well you plan, and how well you execute the plan. The reason the Cowboys were able to put twenty consecutive winning seasons together is because Coach Landry excelled in the area of planning.

Coach Landry had a plan for everything. He had a plan for the offense. He had a plan for the defense. He had a plan for special teams. Honestly, he was the only NFL coach I have ever heard of who put together both the offensive and defensive game plans for his team.

The Cowboys had offensive and defensive coordinators. We had strong coordinators and assistant coaches, and Coach Landry trusted them; but at the same time, he was a very hands-on head coach. He had input in every area of the game.

The Cowboys always had a detailed, comprehensive plan for everything that they did. This was Coach Landry's philosophy: the more detailed the plan, the more likely you will be successful.

That was our philosophy, and I learned a lot from it. Planning puts you in a position to be successful. You do not have to be the smartest, most talented individual in order to be successful, but you do need a plan to be successful.

A plan can get you where you want to go in life. Your talent does not determine your future. You can overcome a lack of talent, but your future is dependent upon your plan. If you do not plan to go anywhere in the future, then you are not going anywhere in the future.

A plan gives you direction. How do you know where you are going without a plan? So many people have no idea where they are going in life because they have no plan. While I was with the Cowboys we always knew where we were going. We always had a plan in front of us that clearly mapped it out. Week after week, year after year, Coach Landry did a great job of developing a plan, presenting that plan to us, and preparing us to execute the plan.

We all need a roadmap in life; without one, it is easy to get off track. Coach Landry never allowed the team to get off track. Now, there were individuals who did at times, but as a team we never got off track. His plan kept us on track.

The plan kept everyone going in the right direction. Even when we struggled, we knew we were going in the right direction because of the plan. We believed in the plan. We had such confidence in the things that we were doing that we never lost faith in the system.

A lot of people outside of the organization lost faith in Coach Landry's system. Fans and the media certainly questioned Coach Landry and his plan early on, but owner Clint Murchison never did. Mr. Murchison trusted Coach Landry and stuck with him.

Everyone inside the organization knew we were moving in the right direction. Everyone, including Mr. Murchison, continued to trust Coach Landry because of the strength of the plan. The plan allowed everyone to know where the team was going and gave us the confidence that it was only a matter of time before we got there. That is what a good detailed plan does; it allows everyone involved to have confidence.

We never lost confidence. We just kept working the plan. Vince Lombardi use to say, "Plan your work and work your plan." That is the key to success. Keep working. Keep fighting. Keep moving forward. Learn from your mistakes. Learn from your losses. If you are going in the right direction, then you cannot allow adversity to steer you off course.

With the Cowboys, that is how we felt as a team early on. We knew we were going in the right direction, so we refused to allow adversity to steer us off course. If we felt like we were getting off course, then we just looked back at our plan. Our plan was our road map, and our road map kept us heading in the right direction.

Coach Landry learned from mistakes and losses as well as anyone I knew. He would always go back and make needed adjustments to the plan. He would not change the plan, but he would make needed adjustments. He was committed to doing everything within his power, everything within his control, in order to put us in a position to win.

Coach Landry would never forsake other responsibilities for the sake of winning a football game. That did not happen. He believed wholeheartedly in prioritizing his responsibilities, which were this: faith, family, and football. Everyone knew that.

His faith in Christ came first, his family second, and football was third. Those were non-negotiable, he did not compromise. He did not allow the demands of football to get in the way of his faith or his family. In my opinion, the reason he was always able to fulfill his responsibilities was because he always had such a detailed plan. He was extremely organized. He managed his time extremely well.

Most successful people do. Most successful people understand that you have to keep your priorities straight. If you lose sight of your priorities, then you end up not being successful at anything. Real success includes keeping your priorities straight. Coach Landry consistently reminded us of that.

Coach Landry was good at reminding us of things. When it came to football, he reminded us that ultimately winning revolves around three things: a plan, preparation and execution. The stronger the three of those are, the stronger you chances of being successful.

It all begins with a plan. Success begins with and is built upon a detailed plan (the more detailed, the better). For Coach Landry, putting a plan together was a tedious process - a slow, methodical, almost pain-staking process, which many people do not have the patience for or the will for. But Coach Landry and the Dallas Cowboys were known for our thoroughness, for our attention to detail.

The Cowboys always had a game plan that would give them a chance to win. There is a lot to learn from that. We all need a plan that will give us a chance to win. Coach Landry's Cowboys had a step-by-step master plan which they prepared for and executed well, which allowed them to be so successful over such a long period of time.

For Coach Landry, everything was series of action steps. He set goals then he developed an extremely detailed plan of how he would accomplish those goals.

Coach Landry said, "Setting a goal is not the main thing, but it is deciding how you will go about achieving it and staying with it (staying with the plan)." He also said, "The secret to winning is constant, consistent management." Coach Landry would create a plan, and then he would keep working that plan and managing the plan until he got it accomplished. That is what allowed the Cowboys to win so many games. That is what allowed the Cowboys to put together twenty consecutive winning seasons.

Lesson Learned

Our goals can only be reached through a vehicle of a plan,
in which we must fervently believe, and upon which we
must vigorously act. There is no other route to success.
—*Stephen A. Brennan*

A plan puts you in a position to be successful; the better the plan the better your chances of success. In life, you need to establish an intended destination, and you need to have directions of how to get there. That's what a plan provides. A good plan includes a destination, and it has step by step directions of how to get there.

You are not going to get anywhere in life if you do not intend on going anywhere in life. If you want to get somewhere, then you need to be intentional about getting there. You have to decide where you want to go and develop a plan of how to get there.

A plan is my means of arriving at a desired destination. In life, I do not get in my car and magically, spontaneously arrive at some random destination. I decide where I want to go, I find directions showing how to get there, then I drive and then I arrive.

The same is true with success. I have to follow the same steps. I need to decide where I want to go in life. I need to find directions on how to get there, and then I need to drive until I arrive at my intended destination. There may be roadblocks along the way, but I am confident that if I keep working the plan, then I will be successful.

Life Exercise

1. Read the quotes at the beginning of the chapter. Reflect on them and then write down the thoughts they bring to your mind.

2. Evaluate your plan. Ask yourself these questions: Do you have a plan? Is it written down? Is it built around your goals? How detailed is the plan? Is it broken down into small steps?

3. Make a decision to put a plan together. You can always add more detail to the plan. But immediately put some plan down in writing. Build the plan around your goals. Have a time frame for the plan. Find someone who has experience putting a plan together and have them help you.

For The Record

Tom Landry is the only NFL coach in the Super Bowl Era to win 13 Divisional Titles. Here is a list of how other all-time NFL great coaches compare.

Tom Landry	Dallas Cowboys	13
Don Shula	Miami Dolphins	11
Bud Grant	Minnesota Vikings	11
Chuck Noll	Pittsburg Steelers	9
Bill Belichick	New England Patriots	9

Timmy Newsome

30 Running Back

Spent 9 years playing with the Dallas Cowboys

Newsome played college football at Winston-Salem State University, where he is the second-leading rusher in school history with 3,843 yards.

He was part of back-to-back undefeated regular seasons at Winston-Salem State in 1977 and 1978. He is also one of the all-time rushers in the Central Intercollegiate Athletic Association. In 1993, Newsome was inducted into the CIAA Hall of Fame.

When drafted by the Dallas Cowboys in the 6th Round of the 1980 NFL Draft, Newsome was a 6'2", 235-pound tailback. At that time, Cowboys Hall of Fame running back Tony Dorsett was in the prime of his career. This forced Newsome to fullback.

Newsome beat out veteran Scott Laidlaw in 1980 primarily because of his versatility. Although he spent the majority of his time playing fullback, he also could play tailback when called upon and tight end as well. He caught the ball out of the backfield exceptionally well, and along with Ron Springs, he filled the role of third down back.

He was the starting fullback for the Cowboys from 1984 to 1988. Before the 1989 season, Newsome went in to visit with new Head Coach Jimmy Johnson. The Cowboys had used a high draft pick on Daryl Johnston that year. Newsome, knowing the Cowboys were embarking on a youth movement, decided it was time to step away from the game.

Throughout the 1980's Timmy Newsome was a clutch player;Newsome contributed greatly to the Cowboys' continued success through the first half of the decade.

Number 09

Develop Daily Discipline

He who lives without discipline dies without honor.
—*Icelandic Proverb*

In reading the lives of great men, I found that the first victory they won was over themselves; self-discipline with all of them came first…If I want to be great, I have to win the victory over myself…self-discipline.
—*Harry S Truman*

Discipline is the refining fire by which talent becomes ability.
—*Roy L Smith*

It was character that got us out of bed, commitment that moved us into action, and discipline that enabled us to follow through.
—*ZigZiglar*

Discipline is the bridge between goals and accomplishment.
—*Jim Rohn*

With self-discipline most anything is possible.
—*Theodore Roosevelt*

Discipline

An activity, exercise, or regimen that develops or improves a skill, the necessary means of attaining goals and dreams, an integral, essential part of success.

Develop Daily Discipline

Interview with Timmy Newsome:

To be successful in Coach Landry's system, offensively and defensively, you had to be willing to work hard on a daily basis. You had no choice. It was such a complex system that was all about precision on both the offensive and defensive side of the ball. The Cowboys had to have guys who had a strong work ethic, and ultimately the key to their success was tied to their ability to find guys who were willing to discipline themselves on a daily basis.

Something I realized from day one with the Cowboys was their commitment to winning. The veteran players on those teams were willing to do whatever was necessary in order to win. You understood that from the first moment you were around those guys.

The Cowboys were used to winning. They had not had a losing season in the previous fifteen years when I arrived. The veterans on the team knew exactly what it took to win. They knew what it took to be successful. They knew the amount of physical and mental preparation that was required in order to be prepared to play and win. They did everything they could do in order to be prepared to play and to win. That was the environment you encountered in the locker room of the Dallas Cowboys, and you had to discipline yourself to the same degree in order to fit in.

A non-disciplined player would not be around for any length of time with the Cowboys. It just did not work. There was simply too much to learn. Not only did Coach Landry have a complex system, but he also had complex game plans. It required complete focus.

Coach Landry did not accept mental mistakes. That is an area you had control over. There are a lot of things you cannot control in football, but you can control mental mistakes. There are a lot of things that can beat you in football, but you cannot allow mental mistakes to beat you. That was Coach

Landry's philosophy.

He knew mental mistakes were a result of a lack of discipline, focus, and mental preparation. With that in mind, the Cowboys were always looking for a certain type of player. They were not just looking for physically gifted players. They were looking for mentally tough, thoroughly disciplined players.

I developed a measure of mental toughness and discipline while I was in college. Coming out of high school, I was 6'2" and 180 pounds. I was a skinny kid who played fullback and safety. The only college opportunity that presented itself to me was at a small university, Winston-Salem State University.

Ultimately, it was a good situation. Initially, I thought I would play defensive back. But at that time, Winston-Salem was running the veer offense, a multiple back set, and they were in need of running backs. So that's where I got a chance to play.

Immediately, I recognized I needed to get into the weight room. I was a long and lean. Actually, I looked frail. I think that is why no other colleges gave me a shot. I had not grown into my body yet. The first thing I had to do was get stronger. The second thing I had to was to put on some weight.

If I could do those things, then I thought I could be successful. It was a challenge, though. It wasn't easy keeping weight on. So for a while, a large part of my time was spent eating and working out. There was a period of time where it seemed like that is all I did.

Fortunately, I had the frame to put on weight, so it was only a matter of me disciplining myself to do the work. I developed a routine. Every day I did something to get stronger and faster. I was in the weight room all the time, and in the end it paid off. My time in the weight room took me from being a frail 6'2", 180-pound fullback and transformed me into 6'2", 230-pound halfback. I got bigger, stronger and faster.

By the time I joined the Cowboys in 1980, having been drafted by them in the 6th round, I was 240 pounds, ran a 4.55 forty, and benched pressed over 400 pounds. All of that, including me getting drafted by the Cowboys, was a result of my developing a daily habit of working hard. When I got to Winston-Salem, I knew that if I was going to be successful on the college level and have a shot at playing in the NFL that I had to work hard every day. Ultimately, it was up to me.

Those years at Winston-Salem provided great preparation for what I would face with the Cowboys, from the standpoint of learning how to be disciplined and work hard on a daily basis. The challenge was different. In college it was a physical challenge, and with the Cowboys it was a mental challenge. Physically, I was ready to play in the NFL; mentally, I was not.

We did not run a pro-style offense in college so everything was foreign to me when I got to Dallas. On top of that, Coach Landry had the most complex offense in all of football. Coach Landry's offense was all about multiple formations. We could run the same play out of as many as four different formations, so there was a lot to learn to say the least.

Immediately after getting the Cowboys' playbook, I knew I would have to apply the same type of daily discipline that I did in college, and even more so in order to get it down. Again, in college it was a physical challenge where I had to work hard in the weight room every day. With the Cowboys, it was a mental challenge where I had to work hard studying and memorizing the playbook every day. And it was a daunting task.

Coach Landry had high expectations. If you wanted a chance to play you had to know the offense well. I had to get this all done as a rookie. When I got there, they had an extremely veteran team. If I could not play as a rookie, then I probably would not make the team.

In other years, the Cowboys had brought some guys along slowly, giving them time to grow into their position. But if I was not ready to play immediately, then they would have stayed with their veterans. The guy I had to beat out was Scott Laidlaw. He was the only true fullback on the team, but he had been there playing for five years.

That provided a great deal of pressure on me and required a great deal of focus from me. I had a large mountain to climb and it was extremely intimidating. It was the most demanding challenge I had ever faced, and it forced me to set everything else aside and completely focus on the objective of learning the offense.

So that is what I did. I was determined to get it done. I was willing to spend as much time as I had to in order to get the offense down. Ultimately, I knew it was up to me. I had the physical skills to play in the NFL, and I knew the Cowboys liked all the things I could do.

The only question was whether or not I was willing to discipline myself on a daily basis in order to internalize the offense and know it well enough to where the coaches had confidence to put me on the field. That is what the

Coach Landry was looking for. The coaches had to know they could trust you.

You had to know all the plays. You had to know all the formations. You had to know all your assignments. You had to know all the adjustments. There was a lot to know.

We might go into a game with say, 120 plays, but each of those plays might be run out of four different formations. So in reality, it was like 500 different plays, and you did not get to practice every play each week. Practices were not long enough to practice every play. Many plays you just had to visualize in your mind. So the mental preparation was extremely demanding.

The bottom line was, you could not be successful playing for Coach Landry unless you were willing to invest the time to be mentally prepared to play. There were other systems in the NFL that were not as complex. There were systems that did not demand as much mental preparation from a player, but not in Dallas.

Coach Landry was confident he could put a game plan together that would allow his team to win more often than not. But he needed a certain type of player to execute his game plan. His system and game plans required smart, disciplined, hardworking, focused, mentally-tough players.

Coach Landry was all of those things. He was the smartest, most disciplined, hardest-working, most focused, mentally tough person that I have ever met. And that was the type of player he was looking for. That was the type of player his system was dependent upon.

The Cowboys were so successful for so long, because they found those types of players. They put together a team of individuals who were willing to discipline themselves on a daily basis in order to achieve certain goals and objectives. Having disciplined players allowed the Cowboys to experience the type of success they experienced.

This is something I have learned in life across the board. I have learned that discipline is the difference between those who do and those who don't. Discipline is the difference between those who are successful and those who are not successful. Discipline makes all the difference in the world. Consistent discipline is the key to accomplishing anything. Coach Landry understood that. The Dallas Cowboys understood that. And that is what allowed us to be so successful.

Lesson Learned

Discipline is the bridge between goals and accomplishment.

—*Jim Rohn*

Without discipline, goals remain nothing more than good ideas. It does not matter how good your plan is if you do not implement discipline, because your goals have no means of becoming a reality.

Success does not happen by accident, and it does not happen by magic. Success comes through hard work. Hard work requires discipline. Discipline allows goals and plans to become accomplishments. Discipline takes me from where I am and moves me to where I want to be. Discipline transports me from point A to point B. Without discipline, I am stuck where I am.

If I want to go anywhere in life, then I have to implement discipline. Success demands discipline. It demands daily discipline. I can't discipline myself sometimes. I have to discipline myself all the time. If I am willing to implement daily discipline, then I can accomplish anything.

Life Exercise

1. Read the quotes at the beginning of the chapter. Reflect on them and then write down the thoughts they bring to your mind.

2. Evaluate your discipline. Ask yourself these questions: How much personal discipline do you have? Are you a disciplined person? Do you develop routines and follow them in order to accomplish goals? In what areas do you need to be more disciplined?

3. Make a decision to improve your discipline. Pick one particular area of your life where you need to be more disciplined, and begin improving in that area. Evaluate your progress. Have someone hold you accountable.

For The Record

The Dallas Cowboys have the most Division Titles in the NFL in the Super Bowl Era with 21. Here is how other NFL teams compare.

Dallas Cowboys	21
Pittsburgh Steelers	20
San Francisco 49ers	18
Oakland Raiders	16
Indianapolis Colts	14
New England Patriots	13
Miami Dolphins	13

Dan Reeves

32 Running Back/ Assistant Coach

Spent 14 years playing and coaching with the Dallas Cowboys

Dan Reeves has participated in more Super Bowls than anyone else in the history of the NFL. He played in two Super Bowls, Super Bowl V and Super Bowl VI, and was an assistant coach in three more:Super Bowl X, Super Bowl XII, and Super Bowl XIII. Reeves was Head Coach in four:Super Bowl XXI, Super Bowl XXII and Super Bowl XXIV as the Denver Broncos' head coach, and Super Bowl XXXIII as the head coach of the Atlanta Falcons.

Reeves was an undrafted free agent with the Dallas Cowboys in 1965. Initially, the Cowboys intended to play Reeves at safety, but out of necessity and because of injuries, the Cowboys moved Reeves to halfback. In 1966, Reeves was pressed into the starting lineup. Reeves led the Cowboys in rushing and was second on the team in receiving. Reeves had 16 touchdowns that year and was voted to the NFL All-Pro team.

Dan Reeves attended college at the University of South Carolina, where he played quarterback from 1962-1964. He was a two-sport star at South Carolina, also playing baseball. Reeves was inducted into the school's Athletic Hall of Fame in 1977.

Reeves spent 23 years coaching for the Denver Broncos, New York Giants and Atlanta Falcons. He is one of the most accomplished and respected coaches of all-time.He played or coached in a record nine Super Bowls – five with the Dallas Cowboys, three with Denver and one with Atlanta. Prior to coaching, he also spent 16 years in the Cowboys organization – five as a player, three as a player/coach and eight as an assistant coach.

Currently Reeves is a broadcaster serving as an NFL analyst for Westwood One.

Number 10

Prepare To Win

Before anything else, preparation is the key to success.
—*Alexander Graham Bell*

A winning effort begins with preparation.
—*Joe Gibbs*

Failing to prepare is preparing to fail.
—*John Wooden*

Good Luck is the residue of preparation.
—*Jack Youngblood*

Confidence comes from preparation everything else is out of our control.
—*Richard Kline*

Never try to be better than someone else. Learn from others, and try to be the best you can be. Success is the by-product of that preparation.
—*John Wooden*

The will to succeed is important... but I'll tell you what's more important: It's the will to prepare. It's the will to go out there every day training and building those muscles and sharpening those skills.
—*Bob Knight*

Prepare

To make ready beforehand for a specific purpose; to study; to practice; to equip yourself to accomplish a specific task, goal or plan.

Prepare To Win

Interview with Dan Reeves:

Nothing is more important to winning than preparation. Preparation is everything, and no one has ever been better in the area of preparation than Coach Landry. His ability to prepare a plan for his team and his ability to prepare his team to execute that plan were the keys to so many victories. There is nothing Coach Landry emphasized more than preparation.

For him, preparation was the greatest motivator. Coach Landry did not use emotion to get a player motivated. He used preparation. Emotion can come and go. Preparation is more concrete. Preparation removes questions, doubts, and indecision from a players mind.

Coach Landry's philosophy was this: if you get a player thoroughly prepared to play, then he will be confident and excited about going out and performing. The greatest thing you can do for a football player or a person in life is to prepare them for success. Conversely, the worst thing you can do is send an individual out there unprepared. Coach Landry never sent his team out unprepared.

Some people may have thought Coach Landry over-prepared, but I would much rather be over-prepared than under-prepared. I guess it all depends on how determined you are to be successful. If you are determined to be successful, then you ought to spend as much time as possible getting prepared to be successful. If success does not mean that much to you, then don't worry about spending that much time preparing.

Our Dallas Cowboys football teams were determined to be successful. That is the type of individual the Cowboys brought into the organization. They brought in individuals who were determined to find a way to win football games. Because they were determined to win, they were also willing to prepare to win.

You have to have determination. You cannot just want to win. You have to be determined to win. You have to have the will to win. You have to be willing to do the things that are necessary to win.

That is the type of player Coach Landry wanted on his football teams. He wanted high character guys, competitors who were determined to win, guys who had the will to win. He wanted guys who were willing to work as hard as they needed to work in order to be prepared to win.

That is the most difficult thing in football. As a coach, or a general manager, or a player personnel guy, the biggest challenge is finding guys who are willing to work as hard as they need to work in order to be successful. That is the biggest intangible in football. It is difficult to measure the size of a guy's heart. You do not always know how hard a person is willing to work in order to be prepared to play and to win.

Some players have a hard time understanding the full value and necessity of preparation, and that can be a problem. That can cause a great deal of frustration for the coaches and the other players who do understand the full value and necessity of preparation.

If everyone on the football team is not on the same page in their commitment to preparation, then inevitably it will cause conflict, which can grow into dissension, which can become a major distraction for a football team. If some guys are working hard to get prepared and other guys are not, then it is going to create a problem.

This was rarely a problem for the Dallas Cowboys. Coach Landry consistently developed leaders who kept the team on the same page concerning preparation. He found guys who took it upon themselves to make sure that everyone on the team was participating in the preparation process. The leaders on the team would set the tone for everyone else.

Everyone needed to be getting the most out of every minute of preparation. That's how you get ready to win. If you do a drill in practice, then you do the drill full speed. If you are in a meeting, then you give your coach your undivided attention. These things make a difference. The leaders on our team made sure those things happened. For our leaders, anything less was unacceptable.

If you were at practice or in a meeting, then you were there for a purpose. The purpose was to get prepared to win. If you were not giving your full effort or your full attention then you were cheating the team.

Some people see those things as being small things; others understand them to be critical things. Some guys just want to get out there and play on Sunday. Others understand you have to spend Monday through Saturday getting prepared to play on Sunday. The difference between winning and losing is small, and the critical deciding factor is preparation

During my time with the Cowboys, which was fifteen years, I never experienced a losing season. My rookie year, we finished 7 and 7; every other year, we finished with a winning record. All of those teams had certain common denominators.

Those teams always had great leadership. Those teams always worked hard as a whole. Those teams were always prepared to play week after week. Our teams were always completely committed to doing whatever we could do to accomplish team goals.

In football, some things are out of your control, but what you can control is how hard you work to be prepared to win. That is in your control. Our teams wanted to win and we were prepared to win. An unwillingness to work and to prepare was never a problem for our teams. Coach Landry made sure of that.

I learned many things from Coach Landry over the years, both personally and professionally. I could spend all day talking about lessons I learned from him, but the two biggest were probably these. First, on a personal level, I learned how to not sacrifice family for football. Coach Landry always scheduled family time with his wife and kids and he did not miss it. Second, on a professional level, I learned how to prepare a team to win.

Ultimately, you can tell how competitive a person is by how hard they are willing to work in order to put themselves in a position to win. Great preparation puts you in a great position to win. How hard a guy is willing to prepare to win will tell you everything about how bad he wants to win.

Coach Landry was the ultimate competitor, and he surrounded himself with ultra-competitive guys. While I was with the Cowboys, I knew that our coaches and our players wanted to win. I knew because of how hard we all worked to prepare to win. This may sound simple but it is true. Winners want to win and they will participate in whatever amount of preparation they have to in order to win.

Winners hate to lose, and they will do anything and everything in their power not to lose. No player wants to lose or likes to lose, but some players are willing to lose. Rather than having a willingness to win, some players have a willingness to lose. In reality, they choose to lose, because they refuse to do everything they possibly can in order to prepare themselves to win.

This was not the case with the Dallas Cowboys while I was there. I was proud to be a part of fourteen of the twenty consecutive winning seasons the Cowboys put together. Nothing was more instrumental to Cowboys' success than their collective commitment to preparation. We always put in whatever amount of work was required to be prepared to win. In the end, the hard work and the preparation paid off.

Lesson Learned

The will to succeed is important…but I'll tell you what's more important: It's the will to prepare. It's the will to go out there every day training and building those muscles and sharpening those skills.
—*Bob Knight*

Success is a by-product of preparation. Success is dependent upon preparation. If you are unprepared, then you will be unsuccessful. The key to victory is preparation.

If you want to win, then you must prepare to win. Preparation facilitates execution. Execution facilitates success. Assurance of successful execution requires your repetitive participation in the preparation process. The act of preparation separates the men from the boys.

Proper preparation puts me in a position to be successful. The more I prepare, the closer I move toward success. There are some things I cannot control in life, but the amount of preparation I put into something is not one of them. Preparation is under my control. If I really want to be successful, then it should be evident in the amount of effort I put into preparation. If I were to fail, it should never be because I failed to prepare.

Life Exercise

1. Read the quotes at the beginning of the chapter. Reflect on them and then write down the thoughts they bring to your mind.

2. Evaluate your commitment to preparation. Ask yourself these questions: Are you preparing yourself to be successful? Are you doing the things that are required of you on a daily basis in order to be prepared to accomplish your goals and plans? How badly do you want to be successful? How hard are you willing to work? Does your commitment to preparation need to improve?

3. Make a decision to improve your commitment to preparation. Determine exactly what things you need to do on a daily basis in order to put yourself in a position to accomplish your goals, and do them on a daily basis. Find someone who is willing to help determine the things you need to do on a daily basis and will also hold you accountable to do them.

For The Record

The following provides a comparison between the Dallas Cowboys' best twenty seasons with Coach Landry and their best twenty seasons without Coach Landry, this time looking at their number of first place finishes.

Dallas Cowboys	1966 – 1985	Division Titles	13
The Dallas Cowboys finished in first place 65 percent of the time.			
Dallas Cowboys	1991 – 2010	Division Titles	8
The Dallas Cowboys finished in first place 40 percent of the time.			

Pat Donovan

67 Offensive Tackle

Spent 9 years playing for the Dallas Cowboys

Donovan spent 1975-1983 with the Dallas Cowboys and was one of the "Dirty Dozen" of rookies who helped the Cowboys to Super Bowl X. Donovan became a starter at left tackle in 1978. He was a four–time Pro Bowler, attending the games from 1979 through 1982.

Sports Illustrated named him the 4th greatest Montana athlete of the 20th Century. In high school, he was a star in basketball, a two-way star in football, and held many state records in track and field. Donovan went to the University of Stanford and was one of the nation's best defensive ends. He was a consensus All-American two years in a row.

The Cowboys switched Donovan to offensive tackle after Rayfield Wright went down with an injury. As a rookie, he took over and helped the team win Super Bowl XII. Donovan emerged as one of the top offensive tackles in the NFL during the late 1970's and early 1980's, and together with Herb Scott formed one of the best left side tandems in the league.

Never missing a game, Donovan played 9 seasons, 20 playoff games, six NFC Championship Games and three Super Bowls, earning a title ring in Super Bowl XII against the Denver Broncos. Donovan is one of the greatest offensive tackles in the history of the Dallas Cowboys franchise.

In 1983, after avoiding major injuries his entire career, he needed surgery to repair both shoulders and decided to retire. Donovan has gone on to develop real estate in his home state of Montana.

Eddie Lebaron the Dallas Cowboys first quarterback flanked by Coach Myers on the left and Coach Landry on the right.

Two of the NFL's all-time greats Cowboys Hall of Fame Defensive Tackle Bob Lilly on the left and Hall of Fame Quarterback Roger Staubach on the right.

George Andrie Cowboys Defensive End reflecting.

Cowboys Guard John Niland

Hall of Fame Tight End Mike Ditka getting on the bus.

Coach Jim Myers Old School Film Room.

George Andrie on the sideline at practice.

Coach Myers at practice.

Cowboys Running Back Dan Reeves

Middle Linebacker Lee Roy Jordan getting ready for action.

D.D. Lewis smiling for the camera.

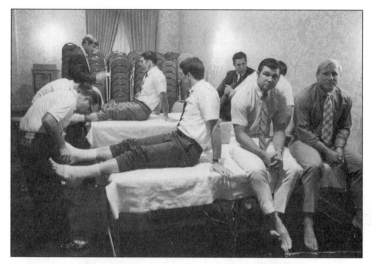

Mike Ditka and Dave Manders waiting to get taped for a game.

*Dallas Cowboys Defensive Lineman, Willie Townes,
Jethro Pugh, Bob Lilly, and George Andrie.*

*Roger Staubach getting a work out
in at practice.*

*Cowboys Running Back Walt Garrison
putting his cleats on.*

Number 11

Evaluate Your Performance

Don't lower your expectations to meet your performance. Raise your level of performance to meet your expectations. Expect the best of yourself, and then do what is necessary to make it a reality.
—*Ralph Marston*

It is our individual performances, no matter how humble our place in life may be, that will in the long run determine how well ordered the world may become.
—*Paul C. Packer*

The man who does not take pride in his own performance performs nothing in which to be proud of.
—*Thomas J. Watson*

Those that are most slow in making a promise are the most faithful in the performance of it.
—*Jean-Jacques Rousseau*

An ounce of performance is worth pounds of promises.
—*Mae West*

A particular shot or way of moving the ball can be a player's personal signature, but efficiency of performance is what wins the game for the team.
—*Pat Riley*

A total commitment is paramount to reaching the ultimate in performance.
—*Tom Flores*

Performance

The result or outcome of preparation; the product of your work; that which reveals where you are; that which ultimately you are measured by.

Evaluate Your Performance

Interview with Pat Donovan:

The Dallas Cowboys developed an extremely detailed system for success. The system was made up of certain individual and team principles. That is, there were certain things we did individually, as players and collectively that allowed us to be successful. One of the things that stood out the most to me within the system was our approach to evaluating our performance. We evaluated our performance, we learned from our mistakes, we found ways to get better, and that process was a large part of our success.

Obviously, there were other teams that did the same things we did. Going in and watching film after a game and evaluating performance was standard procedure in league. But I believe the consistent thoroughness of our process is what allowed us to be one of the top teams in the league year after year.

It was not just a formality. It was not just something we did. It was something we wanted to do. Each of our players bought into the system. We had such a strong locker room full of men who wanted to be the best they possibly could be. So we appreciated the thoroughness of the system. We wanted to consistently and thoroughly evaluate our performance so we could find ways to get better. In order to have real success, you have to have that type of mindset.

Every year we set goals, and we worked hard on a daily basis to reach those goals. Our methodical means of evaluating our performance was one the most valuable tools in helping us move toward our goals.

We did not just watch game tape once a week and review the outcome of the plays. For us, success was not determined by the outcome of the play. Success was determined by us doing what we were supposed to do, the way we were supposed to do it.

Sometimes you can have a successful outcome without doing things right. But most of the time you will not. Most of the time, you will not have a successful outcome if you do not do things the way you are supposed to do them. So when we watched film we were watching every step we took and making sure they were the steps we were supposed to take.

There are times when you have to improvise, but for an athlete that should come naturally. If a play breaks down then, you naturally do what you can do in an effort to end up with a positive outcome. But why did the play break down?

That question defines the importance of evaluating your performance. Why did things break down? Why did the play not work as planned? Why did we not get the desired outcome? Those questions express the need for evaluation.

Doing things exactly the same way over and over again does not come naturally. That is something you have to make yourself do. It is discipline. And discipline is difficult and demanding. We do not naturally make ourselves do difficult and demanding things; we discipline ourselves to do them because they are necessary.

As they rightfully say, "practice makes perfect," or "great practice makes perfect." But in the middle of practice and perfect comes the evaluation of your performance. Each time, you look at what you are doing, and evaluate what you are doing right and what you are doing wrong. You make needed corrections, and you do it again. This allows you to get better and better and better.

It is a painful process. It is not easy at all. Having success in the NFL is not easy. Having success anywhere at anything is not easy. It takes practice. It takes commitment.

But that was the strength of the Dallas Cowboys. Our commitment to success was one of our greatest strengths. If you are not committed then you are not going to get there. We were committed to success. We were committed to excellence. We were committed to do whatever we had to do in order to achieve what we wanted to achieve.

I had to switch positions. I played defensive end in college. I had good size and speed for my position, and I think I could have been successful in the NFL playing on the defensive line. But unfortunately, at least for my desire to play defense, the Cowboys already had two really good young players playing defensive end.

They had Too Tall Jones and Harvey Martin, who were each only in their second or third years. Where the Cowboys were really beginning to need some help was on the offensive line. Both Ralph Neely and Rayfield Wright were going into their ninth and tenth seasons, so the Cowboys were looking for youth at tackle.

Coach Myers, the offensive line coach, was one of the first in the NFL to recognize how important the left tackle position was and always made it a priority to find someone who could play well there. That is where they moved me.

I played behind Ralph Neely for three years while he taught me the position. It was an adjustment, but I appreciated the challenge. I had to learn a new skill set, but many times you have to be willing to change in order to move forward in life.

Changing positions is probably why I had a real appreciation for the way we consistently evaluated our performance, because I needed that. I needed to be looking at what I was doing right and what is I was doing wrong. I needed to review it over and over again. There was a lot to learn, and you had to master it.

The biggest challenge for me was the mental challenge. The physical side of it was difficult; but Coach Landry's offense was so complex and you had to accumulate so much knowledge, which made the mental side of it extremely difficult.

The mental side required more hard work than the physical side did. Coach Landry expected you to know the offense backwards and forwards. And he was always putting in something new. He was an innovator, so there was a lot of studying, a lot of reviewing, and a lot of repetition. Do it, review it, find a way to do it better, and then do it again until you have it mastered.

Coach Landry expected you to master it. That is what the evaluation process was all about. It allowed us to identify the problems we were having in the areas we were struggling in. Once we identified the problem, then Coach Landry could help us fix it. That is what Coach Landry was great at, and that is what our evaluation process was great at - identifying the problem and finding a way to fix it.

For the Cowboys, every part of the process was important. They broke everything down into small steps, and there were not some steps that were important and some steps that were not important. Every step was important. Every step contributed to the success of the team, and the team was committed to every step. It was that type of attention to detail and that sort of fine tuning that exemplified the commitment to excellence which Coach Landry laid as the foundation for the Dallas Cowboys.

As a player and a man, I appreciated it greatly. We all did. We had a great group of guys who believed we could accomplish anything with enough hard work and determination. We all bought into the system. We all encouraged one another to be the best we could be.

If you want to be the best you can be, then you have to consistently evaluate your performance and look for ways to get better. That philosophy allowed the Dallas Cowboys to have a great deal of success; it allowed me to have a great deal of success on the field and off the field as well.

Lesson Learned

Don't lower your expectations to meet your performance. Raise your level of performance to meet your expectations. Expect the best of yourself, and then do what is necessary to make it a reality.
—*Ralph Marston*

In order to master something, you have to prepare, then you have to perform, then you have to evaluate your performance, then you have to prepare some more. That is the routine you have to implement in order to master something. In order to become great at something, you have to participate in a repetitive process that includes the evaluation of your progress and performance.

You do not master something on the first try. It is a process. You learn from your mistakes. The same is true with success; it is a process, and you learn from your mistakes. You consistently evaluate what you are doing wrong and what you are doing right. You make needed adjustments, and you move forward. That is how you become successful.

Taking the time to evaluate my own performance allows me to correct things I am doing wrong. If I never take the time to evaluate myself, then there is the potential to continue to make the same mistake over and over again and find myself falling short of the success I desire to have.

Life Exercise

1. Read the quotes at the beginning of the chapter. Reflect on them, and then write down any thoughts you have.

2. Ask yourself these questions: Do you take the time to evaluate you own performance? Do you run through your mind thinking of what you are doing well and what you are not doing well? Do you have people who can speak into your life, individuals who you can receive constructive criticism from?

3. Make a decision to consistently evaluate you own performance in everything you do. Develop an on-going commitment to excellence. Even though you may never achieve it, pursue perfection at what you do. Master it. Never lower your expectations raise them.

For The Record

From 1966 to 1985, the Dallas Cowboys made the playoffs 18 times in 20 years. No other team has gone to playoffs more frequently in a 20 year span in the Super Bowl Era. Here is how other teams compare.

Dallas Cowboys	1966-1985	18 out of 20 years
San Francisco 49ers	1981-1999	16 out of 20 years
Oakland Raiders	1967-1986	14 out of 20 years
Pittsburg Steelers	1992-2011	14 out of 20 years
Minnesota Vikings	1968-1987	13 out of 20 years
Pittsburg Steelers	1972-1991	12 out of 20 years
Dallas Cowboys	1992-2011	12 out of 20 years
Miami Dolphins	1970-1989	12 out of 20 years
Washington Redskins	1971-1990	12 out of 20 years

Coach Jim Meyers

Offensive Coordinator

Spent 27 years coaching with the Dallas Cowboys

Jim Myers coached 40 years at the collegiate and professional level. Before joining the Dallas Cowboys, Myers was head coach at Texas A&M University.

In 1962, Tom Landry and Tex Schramm went down to College Station and convinced Jim Myers to join the staff of the Dallas Cowboys.

Coach Myers initially coached both the offensive and defensive line. Myers would go on to become the Offensive Coordinator and Associate Head Coach for the Cowboys.

For twenty five years Jim Myers was one of Coach Landry's closest friends. Myers never desired to go anywhere else. All he wanted was the opportunity to compete for a championship, and year after year he got that opportunity with the Dallas Cowboys.

Myers coached in five Super Bowls during his tenure with the Dallas Cowboys.

Jim Myers was the longest tenured assistant coach of the Dallas Cowboys during the Tom Landry era.

Number 12

Commit To Excellence

Excellence can be obtained if you:
…care more than others think is wise;
…risk more than others think is safe;
…dream more than others think is practical;
…expect more than others think is possible."

Excellence is in the details. Give attention to the
details and excellence will come.
—*Perry Paxton*

Excellence is doing ordinary things extraordinarily well.
—*John W. Gardner*

Excellence is the gradual result of always trying to do better.
—*Pat Riley*

No man ever reached to excellence in any one art or
profession without having passed through the slow and painful
process of study and preparation."
—*Horace*

We are what we repeatedly do. Excellence, then, is not an act, but a habit.
—*Aristotle*

Excellence

Surpassing ordinary standards; doing something unusually well; doing something on a superior level; beyond good, beyond great; doing something as well as it can be done.

Commit To Excellence

Interview with Coach Jim Meyers:

The reason the Dallas Cowboys were able to put together twenty consecutive winning seasons was because we were able to find guys who were willing to put in the amount of effort that is required to reach a level of excellence. Excellence is not easily attained. It takes a commitment. You have to be committed to excellence.

Excellence requires a lot of hard work. And the truth that is there are many people who settle for something less than excellence, because they are afraid of the effort and the amount of work excellence requires. Some people do not like to work that hard. Fortunately, in all the years I coached with the Dallas Cowboys and Coach Tom Landry, our teams were never afraid of hard work.

The organization was led by two of the hardest working people I have ever met in my life, Coach Landry and Tex Schramm. Most times in my life, I could outwork just about anybody, but nobody outworked Coach Landry and Tex Schramm. Those two were hard workers.

I know a thing or two about hard work, having grown up on a farm. I don't know if you have ever worked a farm or not, but it requires a lot of hard work. A farm makes you develop a strong work ethic. If you do not work hard on a farm then you are not going to be successful farming. If you do not do things right, then things will not turn out right. You cannot cut corners and have success farming.

The same is true in the NFL. You cannot cut corners and have success in the NFL. If you do not do things right, then things will not turn out right. There is no way around that. You reap what you sow. If you do not sow in hard work, then you will not be reaping much of anything.

Success and excellence demand a commitment to hard work. If your team wants to reach a level of excellence, then the individuals who make up that team collectively have to be willing to put in the required amount of work. The Dallas Cowboys were committed to excellence, and the Cowboys were committed to hard work.

We were led by Coach Landry and Tex Schramm, and those two set the bar for hard work. From day one, those two were absolutely committed to making the Dallas Cowboys a first class franchise. They were a perfect match for one another. They shared a mutual commitment to excellence that you rarely find, and that's what allowed the Cowboys to be so successful.

Coach Landry and Tex Schramm put together an organization that was filled with hard workers from top to bottom. That is what they were looking for. First on their list of qualifications was work ethic. They were not interested in people who were not interested in working hard. You don't need people who will not work hard. They will bring a team down.

On a team, everyone has to pull their own weight, and everyone has to pull in the same direction. People who don't work hard are not pulling their own weight. They are actually pulling in the wrong direction. They pull the team down. People who don't work hard are not working for you; they are actually working against you.

You're either for the team or you're against the team. Players who do not work hard are not working for the team; they are working against the team. In the end, if you do not get rid of people who do not work hard then they will tear a team apart.

Everyone on a team has to be working as hard as they can in order to reach a level of excellence. Reaching a level of excellence is tough. It is difficult. It is not for the fainthearted. If you are faint of heart, then you will quit.

It takes a great deal of mental toughness to overcome obstacles that you are sure to face. But the reality is that if you are going to be successful at anything, then you have to be mentally tough, because you are going to go through difficult times. That is inevitable.

You are going to face a great deal of adversity. That is just a part of it. You have to be ready and willing to fight through adversity. Some guys are willing to quit anytime they get the least bit discouraged. Those guys will never be successful.

Coach Landry knew the type of players he wanted. He wanted players who were mentally tough. He looked for competitors. He looked for hard workers. He looked for fighters. That is really what hard workers are; hard workers are fighters.

Guys who don't work hard are soft. Guys who work hard are tough. Guys who work hard are fighting to be successful. They are fighting to accomplish what they set out to accomplish.

Guys who don't work hard don't care. They don't care if they are successful or not. They would rather quit than fight. They are willing to accomplish nothing rather than fight for something. I was in the Marines; I know a thing or two about fighting for something.

Our Dallas Cowboys' teams were made up of a bunch of fighters. And we were fighting for something. We were fighting to be the best that we could be, and there was no quit in us.

We had a group of men who hated to lose, and we refused to give anything less than our best in order to win. In the end, all you can do is give your best. If you lose while giving your best, then you can live with it. But if you do not give your best, then losing is difficult to live with. All you can do is give your best, and then get back to work and find a way to get better.

That is what we did with the Dallas Cowboys. We did not have success right away, but we always gave our best, and we always looked for ways to get better. We had guys like Bob Lilly, Rayfield Wright, Lee Roy Jordan, and Roger Staubach. All four of those guys were Hall of Famers, and the reason why they were in the Hall of Fame was because they always gave their best and they always looked for ways to get better.

Those four Hall of Famers were what the Dallas Cowboys were all about. They were extremely hard working, driven, and determined to get as much out of themselves as they possibly could. And that is what we did as a team, as an organization. Everyone followed their lead, and we ended up with a lot of hard working guys.

That is what we did as an organization; we worked hard. Why? Because we were driven, determined and committed to reaching a level of excellence. If you are going to do something, then you ought to do it with excellence.

One of the players I was most proud of coaching was Rayfield Wright. Rayfield is a great example of doing something with excellence. When Rayfield first joined the Cowboys, we started him at tight end.

In college, Rayfield was a basketball player - a really good basketball player. He actually could have played professional basketball. He was drafted by Sacramento, but we talked him into playing football. Initially, we did plan on playing him at tight end but then out of necessity we asked him to move to offensive tackle, because we needed someone to block Deacon Jones.

Deacon Jones was a defensive end for the Los Angeles Rams and one of the best defensive ends of all-time. Everybody in the league had a hard time blocking Deacon Jones. He was a beast. He was a big, strong, mean man on the football field.

No one liked going up against Deacon, but we thought Rayfield could do it. Rayfield had such great natural ability. He had the physical talent to be successful at the position, so it was only a matter of whether or not he was willing to put in the work.

We knew that if he worked hard then he could be successful, but you never know how hard a person is willing to work. It turned out that Rayfield was willing to work as hard as anyone. He worked as hard as you could expect a player to work.

Rayfield was a competitor. He was not satisfied with being a good offensive tackle in the NFL. He was determined to be the best offensive tackle in the NFL. That is why he ended up in the Hall of Fame; because he was determined to be the best he could be. He is in the Hall of Fame because of his commitment to excellence.

Rayfield did not coast on his natural ability. He worked as hard as anybody, and his hard work and commitment to excellence allowed him to become one of the greatest offensive tackles of all time. Deacon Jones said Rayfield Wright was the best tackle he ever went up against, and Deacon Jones was a monster.

Rayfield gave a hundred percent all the time. That is what we looked for. We looked for guys who gave a hundred percent all the time. Anything less was unacceptable. You do not reach a level of excellence without giving a hundred percent all the time.

A commitment to excellence is contagious. For us, it started at the top with Coach Landry and Tex Schramm. Those two were determined to surround themselves with coaches and players who shared a common commitment to excellence. We ended up with a coaching staff and a locker room full of players who worked as hard as they possibly could in order to be the best they possibly could be.

That was the key to our success. I stayed around for twenty five years because I did not want to be anywhere else. I had the opportunity to work for world class individuals and a world class organization, and I was loyal. They never gave me any reason to leave, but gave me every reason to stay.

As a coach I wanted to be a part of a winning organization, and ultimately have the opportunity to be a part of a World Championship Team. I got that in Dallas. We did things right, and that allowed us to win often.

We knew if we were loyal to our team principles, then we would be successful. It was all built upon a commitment to excellence and fulfilled through hard work. If you are unwilling to work hard then you will be a failure. You cannot cut corners. You cannot be afraid of the difficult details.

If you want to be successful, then discipline is unavoidable. Winners embrace discipline and hard work. Losers try to avoid them both.

If you do not commit to be excellent then you will never reach a level of excellence. The Dallas Cowboys made a commitment to excellence and we had a great deal of success because of it. Excellence is not arrived at by accident. Excellence comes as a result of doing things excellently.

Lesson Learned

If you do things with excellence, then success will follow. Doing something with excellence means you have put a great deal of work into something. You have practiced and polished your craft. Excellence is not easily attained. Reaching a level of excellence is difficult. It is not accomplished by the faint of heart.

Excellence requires desire, discipline, and dedication. If one is willing to pay the price to attain excellence in anything, then success will be his reward. A commitment to excellence is a commitment to success.

If I am going to take the time to do something then, I ought to take the time to do it with excellence. I can always be proud of doing something with excellence. I can always hold my head high if I do something with excellence. I can feel confident about being successful if I do everything with confidence.

Life Exercise

1. Read the quotes at the beginning of the chapter. Reflect on them and then write down the thoughts they bring to your mind.

2. Evaluate your commitment to excellence. Ask yourself these questions: Do you do everything with excellence? Are you unwilling to do anything halfhearted? Do you do everything to the best of your ability? Do you do things over and over until you get them right?

3. Make a decision to do everything with excellence. Refuse to give any job anything less than your best. Whatever task you do, give it your all. And invest whatever amount of time and energy you have to in order to get it to a level of excellence. Make excellence the standard expectation for everything you do. Never settle for anything less.

For The Record

In the Super Era, the Dallas Cowboys have made the playoffs more years than any other team in the NFL. Here is how other teams compare from 1966-2011.

Dallas Cowboys	30 years in the playoffs
Pittsburgh Steelers	26 years in the playoffs
Minnesota Vikings	26 years in the playoffs
Miami Dolphins	22 years in the playoffs
Oakland Raiders	21 years in the playoffs
St Louis Rams	21 years in the playoffs
Indianapolis Colts	20 years in the playoffs

Tom Rafferty

#64 Offensive Linemen

Spent 12 years playing for the Dallas Cowboys

Tom Rafferty earned All-American honors as an offensive lineman at Penn State University.

Rafferty was drafted in the 4th round of the 1976 NFL Draft by the Dallas Cowboys.

It took Rafferty one year to become the starting left guard, after Blaine Nye retired before the 1977 season. He also performed as a long snapper for field goals and extra points. That team won Super Bowl XII.

During this period, center John Fitzgerald nicknamed the Cowboys' offensive line as the "Four Irishmen and a Scott", consisting of Rafferty, Fitzgerald, Pat Donovan, Jim Cooper and Herb Scott.

Known to his teammates as "Raff," he established himself as one of the better linemen in Cowboys' history, with exemplary work ethic, durability, and versatility. In 1981, he was moved to center after Robert Shaw went down with a knee injury. He became the anchor of an offensive line that would enable the Cowboys' to reach 2 NFC Championship Games.

Rafferty retired at the end of the 1989 season, after rookie Mark Stepnoski became the Cowboys' starting center. He played in 221 total games for the Cowboys, including 167 consecutive games, which at the time was more than any other Cowboy in history. He appeared in 18 post-season games and 2 Super Bowls: Super Bowl XII and Super Bowl XIII.

He was named to the Dallas Cowboys' All-Time Team in 2003. He is the only Cowboys offensive lineman to block for both Roger Staubach and Troy Aikman, and one of only two players, Ed "Too Tall" Jones being the other, to be a teammate of both Hall of Fame quarterbacks.

Number 13

Do Things Right

If you don't have time to do things right, when will you
have time to do things over?
—*John Wooden*

It takes less time to do a thing right than it does to
explain why you did it wrong.
—*Henry Wadsworth Longfellow*

Efficiency is doing things right; effectiveness is doing the right things.
—*Peter Drucker*

Character is doing the right thing when nobody's looking. There are too
many people who think that the only thing that's right is to get by, and the
only thing that's wrong is to get caught.
—*J.C. Watts*

Every job is a self-portrait of the person who does it.
Autograph your work with excellence.
—*Author Unknown*

The truth of the matter is that you always know the
right thing to do. The hard part is doing it.
—*General Norman Schwarzkopf*

Right

The way something is supposed to be done; the proper way of doing things; the best way; the standard of success.

Do Things Right

Interview with Tom Rafferty:

The success of the Dallas Cowboys organization was a result of their commitment to always do things right. There was a certain way the Dallas Cowboys did things. They did things the right way.

The Cowboys did things right in whatever they did. I am sure you have heard people say, "If you are going to do something then do it right, or don't do it all." That was certainly the philosophy of the Cowboys.

When I got to Dallas in 1976, the Cowboys had not had a losing record in ten years. They had only missed the playoffs once in that period of time. They had been to the Super Bowl three times, and had won the World Championship in 1971.

The Cowboys had a core group of veterans who had been there for a while. Guys like Lee Roy Jordan, Ralph Neely, Jethro Pugh, Mel Renfro and Rayfield Wright. Each of those guys had been around for ten years or more, and each of them knew what it took to win.

Those guys were used to winning. They knew what they had to do in order to be successful. If you were going to be a part of the team, then you needed to know how they did things. They had played in a lot of big games. They had lost some, and they had won some, and they knew the difference between winning and losing was small.

The difference between winning and losing any game could hinge on a couple of plays. So you had to do things right all the time, every day you had to do things the right way, in order to put yourself in a position to be successful in those few deciding plays.

With the Cowboys, preparation was everything. They recognized it took the most thorough preparation possible. It took extraordinary effort. It demanded that you disciplined yourself to pay attention to every detail and to practice those things over and over again.

Everyone on the team had to be willing to do those things in order to be a part of the Cowboys. The leadership of the team, both coaches and veterans, made that clear. They set the tone. They set the bar for everyone.

Everyone clearly understood what they were expected to do, and everyone knew they would not be around long if they did not do what was expected of them. You had a job to do, and you were expected to do your job. It was as simple as that.

The philosophy and the expectations were not difficult for me to grasp, probably for a couple of reasons. First, I had already been in a disciplined environment in college. And second, I recognized early on that in order for me to be successful playing in the NFL, because guys were bigger, stronger and faster, I would have to do things right all the time.

In the pros, I was not going to be the biggest, strongest, most athletic guy out there. I wasn't a small guy, nor was I a bad athlete, but I knew that in order to have success against bigger, stronger, faster guys than myself, I would have to have great technique.

That is what I was as a player, I was a technician. Technique was the key for me. I listened to the coaches, I did what they asked me to do, and I did it right. I had to. I was not an overpowering guy. So I had to pay attention to every detail, and then turn around and do that on the field.

In order to put myself in a position to be successful, I had to take the proper steps every time. I did a lot of pulling, so for me to get to certain spots, in order to make certain blocks, I had to do things right.

Small things, but important things, had to happen every time. I had to get the right foot pointed in the right direction at the right time. I had to get my hips turned. I had to get a specific depth behind the line of scrimmage in order to make sure I cleared traffic and got around the end before the running back did.

I had to do those things fast, since I was blocking for Tony Dorsett the majority of my career. When Tony accelerated, it was like he had been shot out of a canon. He could go from standing still to full speed in the blink of an eye.

So if I was going to get out in front of him and make a block, then I had to have perfect technique. I could not afford to waste any steps. It was all about precision and timing. That is why it was all about preparation.

Without thorough preparation you are not ready to play. Thorough preparation requires that you do things right over and over again until it becomes a habit. Then when you go out onto the field on game day you naturally do what you are supposed to do and you put yourself in a position to be successful.

Making a habit of doing things right is what allowed me to be a productive player. It allowed me to contribute to the success of our team. I was productive, and I contributed because I was prepared.

Coach Landry understood and preached the importance of preparation over and over again. We were prepared for every scenario. We covered every detail. Then it came down to execution. And we understood that execution was all about doing things right.

If you want to do things right on Sunday, then you have to do things right Monday through Saturday. For us preparation was everything, preparation was more important than motivation. We had a lot of guys who were self-motivated.

The Cowboys looked for guys who were willing to prepare. Coaches don't have time to motivate players to prepare. If a player cannot motivate himself to prepare then he should not be in the league.

We prepared as well as anyone. We prepared in practice until we got it right. Coach Landry developed a plan for everyone. Everyone was confident that if we did what he asked us to do individually and collectively, then we would be successful.   Obviously we had a lot of success.

We won a lot of football games. Our team was made up of guys who did what was asked of them and expected of them, so that we could win. There were rare exceptions. There were a few along the way who tried to cut corners, but not many. And those guys were not around along.

Players were given a chance to get with the program, or the team would let them move on. Altogether, the Cowboys were extremely hard workers, who did things the same way every time, that we might put ourselves in a position to win, week in and week out.   In the end, we won a lot of games, primarily as a result of doing things right.

Lesson Learned

If you don't have time to do things right,
when will you have time to do things over?
—John Wooden

When I was growing up, I think everyone was familiar with the saying, "Haste makes waste." As a kid, I understood if I did something in haste, that is if I did something quickly, without taking the appropriate time needed to do it right, then more times than not I would find myself having to take the time to do it again.

The saying communicated a fundamental truth: if you don't take the time to do something right, then ultimately you are wasting your time. If you do not take the time to do it right then whatever it is you are doing is not going to come out right. So if you are going to take the time to do something, then you ought to take the time to do it right.

The right way is the best way to do anything. The right way is the standard for success. The right way is the way you do things if you want to be successful. Doing it the right way assures yourself that you will be successful.

Doing things right requires discipline. It is about paying attention to all the little details and then doing them over and over again. I cannot cut corners, and I cannot skip steps if I want to experience success. In football, one will not consistently win without consistently doing things right. The same is true in life. I will not consistently experience success unless I consistently do things right. I have to make a habit of doing things right. When I do, my habit will consistently produce success.

Life Exercise

1. Read the quotes at the beginning of the chapter. Reflect on them and then write down the thoughts they bring to your mind.

2. Evaluate your commitment to doing things right. Ask yourself these questions: Do you try to do things right all the time? Do you have a tendency to cut corners? Do you skip steps sometimes? Do you do things the same way, the right way every time?

3. Make a decision to do things right every time. Give yourself the peace of mind that you did things the right way. Remind yourself that if you do things the right way, then you are sure to get a successful outcome.

For The Record

During the best twenty years under Tom Landry, the Dallas Cowboys made the playoffs 18 out of 20 years. During the best twenty years since Coach Landry the Cowboys made the playoffs 12 out of 20 years.

Dallas Cowboys   1966-1985   Made the playoffs 18 out of 20 years
The Cowboys made the playoffs 90 percent of the time.

Dallas Cowboys   1991-2000   Made the playoffs 12 out of 20 years
The Cowboys made the playoffs 60 percent of the time.

John Fitzgerald

62 Guard

Spent 10 years playing for the Dallas Cowboys

John Fitzgerald was selected by the Dallas Cowboys in the fourth round of the 1970 NFL Draft. In college, Fitzgerald started both as an offensive and defensive tackle at Boston College University.

With the Cowboys, Fitzgerald moved from offensive tackle to center. For the first few years of his career Fitzgerald was primarily a backup to veteran Cowboy center, Dave Manders.

In 1973, after Dave Manders retired, Fitzgerald took over as the starting center for the Dallas Cowboys.

Fitzgerald stayed in the starting lineup for the Cowboys from 1973 to 1980. During that time, Fitzgerald was a part of four Super Bowls.

Throughout his career, he was a central part of a strong Dallas Cowboys offensive line. Fitzgerald named the Cowboys offensive line as the "Four Irishmen and a Scot", referring to himself, Pat Donovan, Jim Cooper, Tom Rafferty, and Herb Scott.

He took great pride in his ability to snap from the Shotgun formation, which the Cowboys re-introduced to the NFL in 1975.

Fitzgerald was the anchor of the offensive line that played in three Super Bowls. The Cowboys made the playoffs every year but once during his career.

Number 14

Do Your Job

Some of us will do our jobs well and some will not,
but we will be judged by only one thing-the result.
—*Vince Lombardi*

Big jobs usually go to the men who prove
their ability to outgrow small ones.
—*Theodore Roosevelt*

Don't be afraid to give your best to what seemingly are small jobs. Every
time you conquer one it makes you that much stronger. If you do the little
jobs well, the big ones will tend to take care of themselves.
—*Dale Carnegie*

Nothing is particularly hard if you divide it into small jobs.
—*Henry Ford*

It isn't about what you do, but how you do it.
—*John Wooden*

Do your job.
—*Bill Belichick*

Job

The specific task an individual takes responsibility for; an amount of work he or she commits to do, is expected to do, and should do with great pride.

Do Your Job

Interview with John Fitzgerald:

With the Dallas Cowboys, everyone understood they had a job to do. It was a business-like environment. It was a business. We each had jobs and responsibilities with the organization. It was still a game, filled with emotion, and it was fun. But at the same time, it was a job. Coach Landry expected everyone to know their job, and he expected everyone to do their job. The reason why the Dallas Cowboys had so much success was because Coach Landry made sure everyone did their job.

If every member on a team takes great pride in doing their individual job, then the collective group will be in a great position to be successful. Coach Landry had extremely high expectations. He expected everyone to their jobs extremely well.

Mediocrity was not something Coach Landry wanted to see. You did not give an average effort, or an ok effort, or even a good effort. That was not accepted. You gave your best effort, or you did not play. We were getting paid to play, and we were getting paid to give our best effort. We were expected to do our jobs to the best of our ability. That was understood by each player.

If an organization wants to be successful, then they have to expect those who make up the organization to give their best effort. If a football team wants to be successful, then every player has to give their best effort. Doing your job includes the expectation to do it to the best of your ability.

Great organizations have high expectations. High expectations are what make organizations great. The Cowboys were a great organization because of their high expectations.

It was a privilege to be a part of the Dallas Cowboys. Being a part of the Cowboys was special. Everyone there recognized that. All of us, regardless of who we were and what our responsibilities were, we each recognized that.

We understood that we each had a role to play within the organization in order for it to continue to be great. Whether you were the quarterback or the place kicker or the equipment manager, you had a job to do. And how well you performed your job had an impact on the success of the team.

Each of us contributed to the success of the team in some way. If you did not contribute something, then you were not kept around. The only way you were kept around is if you found a job to do, and you did it to the best of your ability, and you always looked for ways to do it better.

That was the environment. That was the expectation. That was just the reality. A football team cannot keep guys around just because they are nice guys. A player has to find a way to contribute. For us, it usually began by contributing on special teams and then you had the opportunity to move into other positions. But you had to start somewhere.

From there, you were expected to continue to grow. Regardless of your role, or your area of responsibility, you were expected to work harder, study harder, get better, and find more ways to contribute. That was the expectation. That was the high standard of the Dallas Cowboys.

That is how the Dallas Cowboys became a great organization; because of their extremely high standards. You do not become great without having extremely high standards. Coach Landry always did a great job of clearly communicating the standard.

Everyone knew what was expected of them. We all knew how hard we were expected to work. Others expected it of us and we expected it of ourselves. Each of us expected the guy next to him to find a way to get their respective jobs done. No if's, and's or but's about it - find a way to get your job done.

When I got to the Cowboys in 1971, they had made it to the playoffs five straight years. The year before I got there, the Cowboys went to the Super Bowl and lost to the Colts. They were close to winning it all.

After struggling early on as a franchise, they were close to winning a championship. So when I got there, everyone was determined to find a way to get back to the Super Bowl and win it this time. Everything we did was about finding a way to win it all.

Our job was to work as hard as we could, to make whatever sacrifices that were needed, to pay whatever price that was required, in order to win a championship. We were all on the same page. It was all business.

No one complained. We just went to work. We went about our business the same way every day. You always had to master the fundamentals. You had to do the same things the same way every day, no exceptions and no excuses.

If you want to be something less than the best, then give something less than your best. Join the crowd, make exceptions, make excuses, and settle for being average. But none of that was a part of the Dallas Cowboys.

Special people made up the Dallas Cowboys. Men like Coach Landry and Tex Schramm and Bob Lilly and Roger Staubach - they were special people. I have never seen a group of people work as hard as those guys did, as we did.

It was fun to be a part of it. It was a special group of guys. We always believed we had a chance to win, because we knew how hard we worked to prepare to win. We each worked hard to put ourselves in a position to win.

We were not surprised by our success because we knew we had paid the price to be successful. We were never arrogant, but we were always confidant. There is a big difference.

Our hard work, our preparation gave us confidence. We were committed and prepared to get our jobs done every week. The success of any team is dependent upon each individual getting his own job done.

Our coaches would prepare us to do our jobs and it was our responsibility to get our jobs done. If you did your job then you had the opportunity to be a part of something special. If you did not do your job, then the Cowboys let you move on.

If you did not do your job to the best of your ability, then obviously you did not really want to be there. I found a way to get my job done; I was glad to be there. I played for the Cowboys for ten years, and I am grateful for the experience.

The Cowboys were so good for so long because Coach Landry found guys who were committed to getting their job done. He found guys who willing to do whatever was necessary to fulfill their individual responsibilities.

Excuses were not accepted, and mistakes were not repeatedly made. Our coaches would tell us where to be, when to be there, and what to do when we got there. We were to do it, bottom line.

Today, it seems like excuses are accepted. That was not the case in our day. If you said you were going to do something, then you were expected to do it. If you could not do that, then there was an issue. Coach Landry would point out the problem, discuss it with you, and expect you to resolve it immediately.

There was a clear understanding: do your job or they would have to find someone else who would. That was the reality with the Cowboys. There were firm expectations, high expectations, and those expectations helped the organization to be great.

Lesson Learned

"It isn't about what you do, but how you do it."
—*John Wooden*

Coach Wooden is right. In life, the most important thing is not what you do. The most important thing is how you do it. You do not earn someone's respect because of the job you do, you earn someone's respect by how well you do your job.

Do your job well and others will entrust you with other jobs to do. One of the best things you can do to assure yourself success in life is to do your job to the best of your ability at all times. A job well done will provide you with the opportunity to do another job. If you don't do your job well, you may never get another job. The thought that there will always be another opportunity can be deceiving and destructive.

No one owes me anything in life. If I want an opportunity, then I need to earn it. The reality is that I have to prove myself. I am not entitled to anything. The best way to prove myself to others is to do any and every job entrusted to me to the best of my ability. The best thing an individual can do for me is to expect me to do my job to the best of my ability. When they do that, they set me up for success for the rest of my life. My expectation of myself is to do my job to the best of my ability, always. With that expectation, I can be successful.

Life Exercise

1. Read the quotes at the beginning of the chapter. Reflect on them and then write down the thoughts they bring to your mind.

2. Ask yourself these questions: How well do you do your job? What type of effort do you give on a daily basis? Do you do your job to the best of your ability?

3. Do you believe the following statement by Theodore Roosevelt, the 26th President of the United States? -"Big jobs usually go to the men who prove their ability to outgrow small ones."

4. Does the way you do your job today affect your future?

For The Record

From 1966 to 1985, the Dallas Cowboys played in 20 Championship games in 20 years. They played in 3 Eastern Conference Championship games, in 1967, 1968 and 1969. They played in 2 NFL League Championship Games in 1966 and 1967. They played in 10 NFC Championship games, in 1970, 1971, 1972, 1973, 1975, 1977, 1978, 1980, 1981 and 1982. They won five of those ten games and went on to play in 5 Super Bowls, in 1970, 1971, 1975, 1977 and 1978. Here is a list of the closest three teams in that era.

Dallas Cowboys	20
Oakland Raiders	16
Pittsburgh Steelers	11
Los Angeles Rams	9

Benny Barnes

31 Cornerback

Spent 11 years playing for the Dallas Cowboys

In 1970, Benny Barnes transferred to Stanford University. He was converted from linebacker to cornerback, becoming a two-year starter and part of a defense that helped Stanford win back-to-back Rose Bowls in 1971 and 1972. Although he played just two years, he was inducted into the Stanford Athletic Hall of Fame and selected to the Stanford's All-Century Team.

In 1972, he was signed as an undrafted free agent by the Super Bowl-champion Dallas Cowboys, and made the team based on his excellent special teams play on punt and kickoff coverage.

Barnes did not have great speed, but made up for it with his exceptional balance, instincts and tackling ability. Barnes always played hard and had a knack for making plays.

Barnes played cornerback for the Cowboys in three Super Bowls, winning in 1977.

In 1978, he led the team with 5 interceptions in route to Super Bowl XIII, where he was involved in one of the most controversial calls in Super Bowl history. He and Lynn Swann got tangled up, and Barnes was called for pass interference, giving the Pittsburgh Steelers the ball deep in Cowboys' territory.

In 1981, he was moved to strong safety with the arrival of undrafted free agent, Everson Walls.

Barnes retired after an 11-year career. During his time with the Cowboys, he was part of 8 NFC Championship Games and 3 Super Bowls.

Number 15

Build Your Network

The way of the world is meeting people through other people.
—*Robert Kerrigan*

The quality of your life is dependent upon the quality of your relationships.
—*Anthony Robbins*

It's not what you know, but who you know that makes the difference.
More business decisions occur over lunch and dinner than at any other
time, yet no MBA courses are given on the subject.
—*Unknown Author*

Best results are often achieved well before you need a job, by
consistently networking so that when you find yourself job-
hunting you have a large network to work with.
—*Erik Qualman*

Network

One's collection of business and personal contacts, which has both the potential to create new relationships and the ability to open new doors to needed and wanted opportunities in life.

Build Your Network

Interview with Benny Barnes:

Coach Landry was a class act. People trusted him and respected him. He had a network of friends and business contacts, literally stretched across the globe, which many times provided the Cowboys with the opportunity to find players who otherwise might not have been on their radar. The Cowboys consistently found guys through the recommendation of a trusted contact, which contributed enormously to the success of the organization.

This was my story. I was found and given an opportunity to try out for the Cowboys as a result of Coach Landry's network of friends. Coach Landry was good friends with my college coach at Stanford, Coach John Ralston. After my senior year, Coach Ralston called Coach Landry and convinced him that he should give me a chance to make the Cowboys.

Coach Ralston gave me a good recommendation, letting Coach Landry know what type of player I was and why he thought I could be successful in Dallas. Coach Ralston thought I was a good match for Coach Landry's system, and with that recommendation, Coach Landry decided to give me a shot to make the Cowboys. It was a long shot, but nevertheless it was a shot. It was up to me to make the most of it. You never know where your shot will come from, but whenever it comes, you have to be ready to make the most of it.

It was a long shot because of the amount of talent the Cowboys already had in the secondary. When I arrived for training camp in 1972, there were some huge names on the roster. There were two Hall of Famers in Mel Renfro and Herb Adderly. Then you had Cornell Green, Cliff Harris, Charlie Waters and Mark Washington, who were all extremely talented.

With so many good players in front of me in the secondary, I knew I needed to make myself valuable in other ways and other areas. So what I decided to do was to learn all the assignments and responsibilities of every secondary position. Right corner, left corner, strong safety, and free safety. I learned all the assignments and responsibilities for each position. Anything that I could do to separate myself from someone else, anything I could do to create a reason for them to keep me around, I was going to do.

The other area I focused on was special teams. I knew that could get me on the football team. If I could get on a handful of special teams, then I could make the team. That is what I did. I ended up on almost every special teams unit, and I made the team.

You do what you have to do to contribute. That was my philosophy as a player, always had been. Find a way to contribute. Find a way to make yourself valuable to the team. That is what you had to do, especially if you were going to make the roster for the Dallas Cowboys in the 1970's.

With so much talent on the team already, not just in the secondary but across the board, the Cowboys needed players who could do a handful of things; one, contribute on special teams, two, be ready to play when called upon as a backup, and three, and probably most importantly, they needed players who would not disrupt the existing chemistry of the team.

The Cowboys had worked hard to win their first Super Bowl in 1971. If you were going to make the team then, you had to be a hardworking, "team first" oriented, versatile player, who would fit well in that environment. You had to have the right attitude. You needed to be willing to do whatever it took to contribute and whatever it took to fit in.

That worked well for me, because I was that type of player. Whatever it took to contribute, I was willing to do. Wherever my coach needed me to play, I would play.

In high school, I played linebacker. In college I played safety. And in the NFL, I ended up primarily playing cornerback. My attitude was that wherever the coach thought the team needed me, I would play, and that attitude served me well. My attitude was a big reason why my college coach and coaches before that went to bat for me.

My coaches knew I would do what they asked me to do. That was honestly the key to my success, especially with the Dallas Cowboys. I didn't have great speed to play secondary in the NFL. I probably ran just under a 4.7 in the 40 yard dash.

Coach Landry's system actually made things easier. If you studied and you knew your assignments and your responsibilities, then you would be successful. He always put you in a position to be successful. As long as you put in the work to be prepared, then the system would put you in a position to be successful.

I was willing to work and study and prepare as hard as I needed to. Whatever I needed to do, I was willing to do. For that Coach Landry kept me around for 11 years. I had a good relationship with Coach Landry because I did what was expected of me, and his system allowed me to be a productive NFL player. It allowed me to part of the success of the Dallas Cowboys.

I could not have ended up in a better place. Dallas was the right place at the right time. I got the chance to be a part of something special. And ultimately, I have my college coach, John Ralston to thank for that. He thought enough of me to take the time to talk to Coach Landry on my behalf. I had earned my coaches' trust by doing whatever they needed me to do and it paid off in a big way.

Fortunately, every time I needed a chance to prove myself at the next level in football, I got one because of my previous coaches. When I finished high school I didn't know if I would have a chance to play college. I was a linebacker in high school, but I wasn't big enough to play linebacker in college, and there were questions about whether I was fast enough to play secondary on the college level.

But my high school coach was friends with the head coach of Contra Costa College, a local junior college, and I got a chance to play there. I made the most of it. I was a very productive player at Contra Costa, and my coach there, Vince Maiorana, was friends with John Ralston, who was the head coach at Stanford.

Coach Maiorana told Coach Ralston that he should give me a chance to make the team at Stanford. Coach Ralston did. I ended making the team, and I started both my junior and senior year. Both of those years we played in and won the Rose Bowl.

Ultimately, my career opportunities were presented to me as a result of my relationships. My network, my trusted relationships, opened up opportunities for myself at critical moments. My coaches knew I was a hard worker. I had to be. Nothing ever came easily for me. I did what my coaches asked me to do. I found a way to contribute, and I contributed as much as I could.

Coaches knew that they could count on me. My teammates knew they could count on me. I try to make sure everyone around me knows they can count on me. I have found that if you have a reputation as someone who will always do what they say they will do, and if you will do what others ask you to do, then your reputation and the recommendation of others will open up opportunities for you at different times in life

In life, as you meet people you cannot take your relationships for granted. You have to value your relationships. You never know what impact any of your personal relationships may have on your life. In life, you reap what you sow. When you treat people with respect then you earn people's respect. When you look out for others then others look out for you.

You have to always maintain your relationships. You have to earn people's trust, and you have to maintain their trust. When you do, you develop a reputation as someone who can be counted on. If you consistently meet people's expectations as a hard worker, then it is only a matter of time before your relationships create opportunities.

For years, the network of Tom Landry worked for the Dallas Cowboys. I was just one example of the Dallas Cowboys finding productive players through the recommendation of a friend or contact of Coach Landry. People close to Coach Landry knew the type of players he was looking for, and they consistently sent those types of players his way. Those players helped the Dallas Cowboys put together twenty consecutive winning seasons. I was fortunate enough to be one of those players.

Lesson Learned

In life, as you meet people, you cannot take your relationships for granted. You have to value your relationships. You never know what impact any of your personal relationships may have on your life.

In life, you reap what you sow. When you treat people with respect then you earn people's respect. When you look out for others then others look out for you.

In my pursuit of success, I must be diligent and disciplined in maintaining my relationships. I have to earn people's trust, and I have to maintain their trust. When I do, I develop a reputation as someone who can be counted on. And when I consistently meet people's expectations as a hard worker, then it is only a matter of time before my relationships create needed and wanted opportunities in life.

Life Exercise

1. Read the quotes at the beginning of the chapter. Reflect on them, and then write down the thoughts they bring to your mind.

2. Ask yourself these questions: Do you take the time to build relationships? Do you have a good reputation with others? Would others go out of their way to help you? Are you trustworthy, do you always do what you say you are going to do?

3. Make a decision to be more intentional about your network. Look for times and places to meet new people. Value all of your current relationships. Be consistent. Earn people's trust. Give no one any reason to speak poorly of you.

For The Record

In the Super Bowl era, there are three coaches who stand above all others: Tom Landry, Head Coach of the Dallas Cowboys, Chuck Noll, Head Coach of the Pittsburgh Steelers, and Don Shula, Head Coach of the Miami Dolphins. Here is a comparison each of the coach's best twenty seasons, specifically looking at the number of times each coach put his team in a Championship game, with the opportunity to play in the Super Bowl.

Tom Landry	1966 – 1985	12 Championship Games
Chuck Noll	1972 – 1991	7 Championship Games
Don Shula	1970 – 1989	6 Championship Games

Alicia Landry

Beloved Wife of Tom Landry

Enjoyed 51 years of marriage to Tom Landry

As a 17-year-old University of Texas freshman, Alicia Wiggs went on a blind date with Longhorn junior defensive back and fullback, Tom Landry. The two would end up going on a date every week for the next 53 years.

Two years, later Alicia Wiggs would become Mrs. Alicia Landry. Tom and Alicia Landry enjoyed 51 years of marriage before Tom Landry's passing in 2000.

Alicia and Tom spent the first years of their life together in New York, with Tom playing and coaching for the New York Giants. The two enjoyed a wonderful relationship with the Mara family, and could have coached long-term with the Giants, but the Landrys wanted to move back to Dallas.

Alicia, a native of Highland Park, was ready to go back home. As it would turn out, at the same time the Landry's were intending to move back to Texas, the Dallas Cowboys' franchise was coming to life.

Clint Murchison was awarded the rights to start a football team in Dallas, and his desire was for Tom Landry to be his head coach.

In 1959, Murchison made Tom and Alicia Landry an offer they could not refuse, and the two moved back to Dallas. There they enjoyed a Hall of Fame career with the Dallas Cowboys. Tom always welcomed input from one of the most gracious, well-respected individuals in Dallas, his wife Alicia Landry.

Alicia and Tom had three children: one son, Tom Jr., and two daughters, Kitty and Lisa.

Number 16

Be Extremely Organized

You've got to stop dividing yourselves. Yougot to organize.
—*H. Rap Brown*

Whether you're a newspaper journalist, a lawyer, a doctor.
You have to organize your thoughts.
—*Frederick Wiseman*

"Organize your life around your dreams - and watch them come true."
—*Unknown Author*

If you can organize your kitchen then you can organize your life.
—*Louis Parrish*

Don't agonize, organize.
—*Florynce R. Kennedy*

For every minute spent in organizing an hour is earned.
—*Unknown Author*

Organizing is what you do before you do something,
so that when you do it, it is not all mixed up.
—*A.A. Milne*

Organized

Efficient, methodical, planned, structured, control of direction and activities.

Be Extremely Organized

Interview with Alicia Landry:

The Cowboys coaches did a great job of prioritizing their responsibilities. They managed their time well. They did not waste their time. All of which were a result of how organized they were. As a team, they had great organizational skills, and I believe that contributed as much to their success as anything.

The Dallas Cowboys were an extremely organized franchise. The leadership made sure of that. They put together a wonderful team of people and the team worked well together.

Everyone understood their role within the organization and everyone focused on their role. There was so much work to be done, and there was so much that went into the preparation process. I always heard about coaches in the NFL who basically lived out of their offices, but I did not see that with the Cowboys.

My husband, Tom Landry, who I personally called "Tommy," was an extremely organized individual himself. He focused on the things that needed to be focused on. He had the ability to zero in on the things that were really important.

He was efficient and effective with his time. He had to be. He had a lot of responsibilities. Being head coach of the Cowboys demanded a great deal of his time, but he never sacrificed his family for football. We always had regular family time. He worked reasonable hours, and then he was home and available. He was never absent.

Tom always had breakfast with the family, and we didn't eat dinner until he got home. He did have a projector in his office at the house, and he would spend time in there, but he stayed engaged with the family. He never closed himself off.

At times, he would have other coaches come over to the house and work. They would sit at the dining room table and draw up plays. Our first dining room table was wood, and they almost ruined it. I had to get a glass table. But that did not happen a lot, and it never interfered with our regular family time.

The Cowboys as an organization had a great family atmosphere. They made sure they kept everything in perspective. Tom had three priorities in life, in this order: faith, family, and football. He encouraged everyone to maintain those priorities, and the Cowboys as a whole did a good job of that.

Tom looked for players who could keep their priorities straight. That was important. Whether or not a person can keep his priorities straight says a lot about the individual.

Tom was always looking for players who had certain attributes. He wanted players with great discipline. He looked for individuals who wanted to excel. He looked for guys who were intelligent. Most of all, he was interested in strong character. He looked for strong men, because strong men keep their priorities straight.

For Tom, keeping his priorities straight and taking care of all of his responsibilities were dependent upon him managing his time well and being extremely organized. And Tom was good at both.

He recognized there was only so much time in a day, so he had a plan detailing how he would manage his time. In order for him to make sure he spent the amount of time he needed to spend in the areas that deserved and demanded his attention, he knew he had to be extremely organized.

Without being organized, there would have been no way for him to do everything he needed to do. If he was not organized, then some things would have fallen through the cracks. For Tom, that was unacceptable.

Tom expected the players to be organized as well. They had to be in order to be successful with the Cowboys, because the Cowboys were so regimented. In order to get everything done that needed to be done each week, players had to develop a strict routine.

Players had to be where they needed to be, when they were supposed to be there. They needed to be on time. They needed to know what they were expected to know when they got there. If they didn't, then that was a problem. Everyone needed to be on time, and everyone needed to know their assignments. Players had to manage their time well.

If a player was late for a meeting, or they did not know their assignments, then that affected the whole team. It was disrespectful to the whole team. Everyone on the team was supposed to be committed to doing everything they could to help the team win.

Tom was a perfectionist. He took great pride in everything he did. He felt that if you were going to do something, then you ought to do it right. He certainly did. He did not understand any other way of doing things. He was absolutely committed to excellence in everything he did.

He looked for players who shared his commitment to excellence and he found them. He found guys who were committed to excellence. He found guys who were committed to doing things a certain way. The Cowboys had a great group of guys who were committed to being the best they could be. They all understood that everything they did had a purpose and the purpose was to win games.

Tom liked to win. He was the most competitive person I have ever known. It didn't matter what he played; for him the reason you played was to win.

I remember one time, Tom was teaching our little boy, who was only seven at the time, how to play a board game. So Tom sat down and explained the rules to Tom Jr. and then said, "Remember, the point of the game is to win." I almost fell out of my chair. I was sitting there thinking the point of a board game was to have fun. But that was not the case for Tom. The point of the game for Tom was to win.

If you did everything you could do to win and you still lost, then Tom could live with that. It was never easy for Tom to lose, but if he and his team had given their best then he could live with it.

For Tom, making the most of your time was the key to giving your best. You only had a certain amount of time to get prepared and if you didn't make the most of that time then you were not giving yourself the best chance to be successful.

Tom firmly believed that the team which was most prepared to play would be most likely win. So you had to make the most of the time; you had to prepare. And in Tom's mind, the way you made the most of the time you had to prepare was by being extremely organized.

Tom thought everything through. He went through the process in his mind a number of times before he put something down on paper. His degree was in Industrial Engineering. He spent a lot of time processing information and figuring out how things work best. He would always find a way to maximize the effectiveness of anything he touched.

I believe the additional amount of time he took to think things through, in the end actually saved him time. Tom was smart. He always took the time to develop a plan, and the plan would ultimately save time.

Tom did not like to waste time. There were too many things that he was committed to; he could not afford to waste time. He liked to be organized, and he had to be organized. He felt if you were not organized, then you were scattered. You cannot be real effective at anything if you are scattered.

Tom was never scattered. He was always focused. He was the most focused individual I ever met. He always took the time to gather his thoughts, and then he formulated a plan. Nothing was random with Tom. He was always intentional and strategic. All of those things played a large role in his success as a coach.

His teams were always strong in those areas. The other coaches and the players on those Cowboy teams were always focused. As an organization, they were all very organized. Everything was broken down into small steps. The team had goals and objectives that were all a part of an extremely detailed plan, that was clearly communicated to everyone involved.

Tom believed the biggest key to winning was preparation, and a critical component of preparation was organization. The more organized you were, the better prepared you could be. Organization and preparation produced precision. And football is all about precision.

Being extremely organized gave Tom and the Dallas Cowboys the best chance of being successful. Their organizational skills played a large role in their success. They managed their time well, and they were as thoroughly prepared as possible week after week. That put them in the best position to win, and they won a lot. For twenty straight years they always won more than they lost.

Lesson Learned

Getting the most out of life requires you to be extremely organized. The more organized you are the more you can accomplish. Being organized allows you to have a clear view of what you need to do next in order to be successful.

When your life is cluttered and unorganized, there is potential to get lost in it all. It is hard to see the steps you need to take in order to move toward your goals. Being organized makes success easier. Being unorganized makes success more difficult. I do not need to add any additional difficulty to my pursuit of success.

My goal is to be as organized as possible, to methodically move step by step toward success. Being organized allows me to make the most of my time. The more time I have to invest in the pursuit of my goals the better. Life is short. I need to make the most of every moment. Being organized allows that to happen.

Life Exercise

1. Read the quotes at the beginning of the chapter. Reflect on them and then write down the thoughts they bring to your mind.

2. Ask yourself these questions: How organized are you? Do you schedule your time regularly? Do you keep the space around you orderly? Do you have a disciplined, daily routine that helps you accomplish specific tasks?

3. Take some steps to become more organized. Plan your time each day. Organize your room, your office, your car. Clear out all the clutter in your life physically and mentally.

For The Record

Coach Landry led his team to a Championship Game with the opportunity to play in the Super Bowl more times than any other NFL Coach in the Super Bowl era. Here is how other NFL-greats compare.

Tom Landry	12 Championship Games
Don Shula	8 Championship Games
Chuck Noll	7 Championship Games
Bill Belichick	6 Championship Games
Bill Cowher	6 Championship Games
Bud Grant	5 Championship Games

John Niland

61 Guard

Spent 9 years playing for the Dallas Cowboys

John Niland was drafted in the first round, fifth overall, of the 1966 NFL Draft by the Dallas Cowboys. He became the starting left offensive guard for the Cowboys from 1966 to 1974. One of the top offensive lineman of his era, he was particularly excellent as a pulling guard.

Practicing against Bob Lilly from his rookie year helped him become a Pro Bowler and solidified an offensive line that won 2 NFC Championship Games and 1 Super Bowl.

The Cowboys made the playoffs every year except Niland's last, in 1974. While Niland was there, the Cowboys played in 6 Championship games and 2 Super Bowl's.

As a rookie in the 1966 NFL Championship Game the 1967 NFL Championship Game(the so-called Ice Bowl), both Cowboy-losses to the Green Bay Packers, Niland played left offensive tackle.

In 1975, John Niland was traded to Philadelphia for a third round pick. The Cowboys used the selection to draft wide receiver, Tony Hill.

Along with Rayfield Wright, Nate Newton and Larry Allen, Niland is one of only four offensive lineman in team history with at least six Pro Bowl selections. He was selected to six consecutive Pro Bowls from 1968 to 1973 and was a three-time All-Pro selection. Niland only missed two games in his nine seasons with the Cowboys.

Number 17

Be Completely Confidant

Confidence is contagious. So is lack of confidence.
—*Vince Lombardi*

Optimism is the faith that leads to achievement.
Nothing can be done without hope and confidence.
—*Helen Keller*

Confidence... thrives on honesty, on honor, on the sacredness of obligations, on faithful protection and on unselfish performance.
Without them it cannot live.
—*Franklin D. Roosevelt*

Life is not easy for any of us. But what of that? We must have perseverance and above all confidence in ourselves. We must believe that we are gifted for something and that this thing must be attained.
—*Marie Curie*

Inaction breeds doubt and fear. Action breeds confidence and courage. If you want to conquer fear, do not sit home and think about it.
Go out and get busy.
—*Dale Carnegie*

Believe in yourself! Have faith in your abilities!
Without a humble but reasonable confidence in your own powers, you cannot be successful or happy.
—*Norman Vincent Peale*

Confidence

Belief in oneself, a trust in your preparation, the belief in your own ability to get a job done; being certain in your ability to accomplish a specific task.

Be Completely Confidant

Interview with John Niland:

The Dallas Cowboy teams I was a part of had a great deal of confidence. Some people viewed us as being over-confident or arrogant, but that was not the case. We were just confident. We were completely confident in our ability to go out and win week after week, and that confidence was a huge part of our success.

We had a number of reasons to be confident. One, we had a great deal of talent on our teams. Two, we had great deal of leadership on our teams. And three, we did a great job in the area of preparation on our teams.

When you are strong in those three areas, then you feel pretty good about your chances of winning. We were especially strong in the area of preparation. I think that was probably the most important of all. We prepared well and that preparation gave us confidence

Confidence affects your performance. If a player starts to lose his confidence, then his performance will drop off. In order for an individual to play up to his full potential at the highest level, he has to have complete confidence in his talent and his preparation.

I can have all the talent in the world, but if I am not prepared, then I am not going to be successful. The amount of confidence I have in myself should be proportionate to the amount of time I have put into preparation. If I am not prepared, then I should not be confident. If I am well prepared, then I should be confident.

I was always confident in my ability to go out and win individual match ups, and that was directly related to the confidence I had in my preparation. Somewhere along the way, I read a book called "Psycho Cybernetics" by Dr. Maxwell Maltz. The emphasis of the book was the power of visualizing something in your mind.

The book talked about the benefits of mental visualization, and I bought into it and made it a vital part of my preparation. Every week, as I got prepared for a game, I would visualize myself in my mind making every block I needed to make. I would walk through every play in my mind and see myself successfully blocking my man every time. It may sound crazy but it worked. It helped me a great deal.

Preparation removes questions, doubts, and indecision from a players mind; there is no time for any of those. There is certainly no time for any amount of indecision in the NFL. You have to be decisive at all times. You have to be confident at all times.

You have to know what you are going to do in every situation of a game. Everything has to become second nature. The team that does the best job of that is going to win more often than not. When you have complete confidence that you can do it, then you should do it. If you are completely prepared to do it, then you should do it.

Coach Landry believed the greatest motivator was preparation. He felt that if a player was thoroughly prepared to play, then he would be confident and excited to go out and play. I think Coach Landry was right. Competitors love to go out and show what they can do. They love to go out and do what they do to help their team win.

The only reason a competitor would not be excited to play is if for some reason he was not prepared to play. When you are completely prepared, then you should be completely confident. That was the case with our teams. We were prepared, confident, and excited to go out and perform.

We went into a game knowing what we were going to do. We had already done it hundreds of times in our minds, during meetings and on the practice field. We knew what our opponents were going to do. We knew what adjustments we might have to make. We knew what adjustments we would have to make to their adjustments.

When game-time came, we were as prepared as we could be and we trusted our preparation. If we struggled early on in a game, we didn't question ourselves or our ability to win; we just kept doing the things we had practiced, and believed it was only a matter of time before we started having success.

That is why we never thought we were out of a game, and why we had so many comeback victories. We had a great quarterback in Roger Staubach (who was nicknamed "Captain Comeback"), and we had great confidence in him, but we also had great confidence in our preparation. Our complete confidence in ourselves and our preparation convinced us that regardless of how things looked, if we continued to do the things we were supposed to be doing, then in the end we would win.

We always knew how hard we had worked, and we were confident that our hard work would eventually pay off. That is one of the things that impressed me the most about our teams. If we struggled, we did not get down or doubt ourselves. We just kept fighting. We kept battling.

The year we won our first Super Bowl, we actually got off to a pretty rough start. We were only a game above five hundred half way through the season. We had almost lost as many games as we had won. We had high hopes for that year, and it didn't look like we were going to live up to them. But we didn't give up on our goals. We regrouped.

If we would have lost our confidence, then everything would have come apart. But we didn't allow that to happen. We refocused ourselves, believing things would turn around, and they did. We didn't lose another game that year. We went all the way to the Super Bowl and won it.

The reason why we were able to overcome the early adversity of that season was because we were so confident in our ability. We always believed we were going to win. You have to. You can't go into a game thinking you are going to lose. Your outlook has an effect on the outcome.

When I joined the Cowboys in 1966, they had a good team. They struggled the first few years, but they had made the playoffs the year before I got there. From there, they put together twenty consecutive winning seasons. While I was with the team, the Cowboys made the playoffs every year other than my last. In that era, the Cowboys made the playoffs nineteen times out of twenty one years. That was an amazing accomplishment, and the key to it was confidence.

The Cowboys developed a formula for success, and we had a great confidence in the formula. We knew it worked. The formula included talent, leadership, hard work, thorough preparation and confidence. We had those things.

We were talented, and we had great leadership. Our leadership made sure that we worked extremely hard. They made sure we were thoroughly prepared, and those things provided us with confidence. We were not overly confident. We just had complete confidence in our ability to go out and win.

We did not doubt ourselves. We believed in ourselves, and we experienced a great deal of success. The Cowboys put together a stretch of success that no other team has matched to this point.

Lesson Learned

Confidence is contagious. So is lack of confidence.
—*Vince Lombardi*

A lack of confidence in your own ability can prevent you from attempting to accomplish certain things in life. Nothing can be more distracting and destructive to accomplishing goals than a lack of confidence.

Success at anything in life is not easily attained. A mental battle takes place in your own mind every day as you work to make your dreams come true. As each day goes by, a lack of confidence will work to convince you to quit. On the other hand, confidence in your own ability will work to convince you that you can and that you can accomplish anything that you set out to do.

Confidence is not arrogance, confidence is crucial. A lack of confidence tells our minds we can't. Confidence tells our minds we can. Confidence is an essential part of success. If I take the needed and necessary time to plan and prepare for a specific task then I should be completely confident in my ability to accomplish it. Confidence energizes my mind and body.

Life Exercise

1. Read the Quotes at the beginning of the chapter. Reflect on them, and then write down the thoughts they bring to your mind.

2. Ask yourself these questions: how confident are you in yourself? Do you believe you can accomplish anything you set your mind to? Is your confidence in line with your preparation for a particular task?

3. Make sure you have a healthy measure of confidence in yourself and your ability to achieve a specific task. If you are prepared for it, then be confident about it. Rid yourself of any lack of confidence.

For The Record

The Dallas Cowboys' 12 Championship games, between 1966 and 1985, are more than the combined total of 12 teams over the same amount of time. This includes all of their NFC East foes.

Washington Redskins	3
New York Jets	2
Green Bay Packers	2
New England Patriots	1
Cincinnati Bengals	1
Buffalo Bills	1
Philadelphia Eagles	1
New York Giants	0
Atlanta Falcons	0
Detroit Lions	0
Arizona Cardinals	0
Cleveland Browns	0

Bill Glass

80 Defensive End

Enjoyed 40 years of friendship with Coach Landry

On the football field, Bill Glass was a defensive end who played eleven seasons in the National Football League, beginning with the Detroit Lions and finishing his career as a standout with the Cleveland Browns.

Glass played college ball at Baylor University, where he was one of the country's best defensive linemen. He lettered three years at Baylor University, 1954-56, and was unanimous All-American guard in 1956. He made 154 tackles in 10 games and was elected to the College Football Hall of Fame

His pro career included one year with Saskatchewan in the Canadian Football League in 1957. Then he played four years with Detroit (1958–61) and seven years with Cleveland Browns(1962-68).

Glass started for seven years with Cleveland. He became a Pro Bowl defensive end with the Browns, playing a key role in the team's NFL championship in 1964 and Eastern Division championship in 1965. He retired after the 1968 season.

After retiring from football, Bill Glass started a national prison ministry. Bill Glass Ministries visits prisons all over the country.

Number 18

Control Your Emotions

Take control of your consistent emotions and begin to consciously
and deliberately reshape your daily experience of life.
—*Tony Robbins*

Control your emotion or your emotion will control you.
—*Unknown*

Self-discipline begins with the mastery of your thoughts. If you don't
control what you think, you can't control what you do. Simply, self-
discipline enables you to think first and act afterward.
—*Napoleon Hill*

When we direct our thoughts properly, we can control our emotions.
—*W. Clement Stone*

No one can make you jealous, angry, vengeful, or greedy-unless you let him.
—*Napoleon Hill*

Regardless of how you feel inside, always try to look like a winner. Even if
you are behind, a sustained look of control and confidence can give you a
mental edge that results in victory.
—*Arthur Ashe*

Nothing gives a person so much advantage over another as to
remain always cool and unruffled under all circumstances.
—*Thomas Jefferson*

Control

The ability to manage one's conduct; to act wisely and appropriately; to hold in check, to show restraint; to have authority over a situation.

Control Your Emotions

Interview with Bill Glass:

Coach Landry's ability to control his emotion helped the Dallas Cowboys win a lot of football games. In football, if a player or a coach allows emotion to get the best of him, then it can have a negative impact on the team. An unsportsmanlike conduct penalty alone costs you fifteen yards, and that is hard to overcome. That is just one part of it. If you cannot control your emotion, then at some point in time your emotion is going to control you. Coach Landry did not allow this to happen to himself, and rarely did he allow it to happen to his football team. Coach Landry's teams were always focused and under control, which allowed them to win a lot of games.

Every person needs to learn to control their emotion; at some point, their emotion will become a major distraction for them if they don't. In football this is especially true. In football, the emotion of one play can negatively affect the outcome of another. If you get all upset over the previous play, then it can keep you from focusing on and being successful in the following play. Coach Landry did not allow himself to be in that position. He was always able to focus on the next play. He was always in control of his emotion. He was the best at it, and his unique ability to control his emotion was a key component to the success of the Dallas Cowboys.

For years, a lot of people, especially the media, spent a great deal of time describing Coach Landry as unemotional. Over and over again, they would show this stoic image of him pacing the sideline. They portrayed him to be some kind of machine. But that was not the case at all.

Coach Landry had plenty of emotion. He was a fierce competitor. And competitors are emotional. Competition is filled with emotion. NFL players thrive on it. They rely on it. But great competitors know how to control it. Coach Landry's ability to stay calm and stay focused on the objective of the moment led others to conclude that he was stoic, but he wasn't. He was just under control and focused.

Coach Landry flew planes in World War II. He was a bomber pilot. On one particular mission, his plane was hit by enemy fire. This caused his engines to go out, and with the plane having no power, everyone on board began preparing to evacuate the plane.

Yet, Coach Landry continued to go through his system checks looking to find a way to get the engines started again. Finally, with everyone at the door of the plane ready to jump out, Coach Landry got his parachute ready. But before he let anyone jump he decided to do one last system check. Even in that type of emotional moment, he was able to gather himself, and he was able to continue to process information throughout the situation.

In the end, he was able to get the engines started again. Everyone went from jumping out of a plane over enemy territory to landing safely in the intended ally landing area because of Coach Landry's uncanny ability to focus. It's a great story, and it's a perfect example of how he had the ability to control his emotion. Nothing ever rattled him. He was always cool, calm and collected.

Coach Landry was able to continue to process information with amazing effectiveness, even in the most difficult circumstances. This served him well in football because in football, you have to be strategically thinking at all times. Players and coaches have to have their heads in the game at all times. Coach Landry always did. He was the most focused individual I ever met.

One time I spoke on focus at a Cowboys chapel service, and I used this analogy. I said, "If I took a two-by-six board and placed it on the ground, and asked you guys to walk across it, then any of you could. A two-by-six board is plenty wide to comfortably walk across. No one in this room would have a hard time doing that. But if I laid that same two-by-six across two twenty-story buildings and asked you guys to walk across it, then I do not know if anyone in this room would or could do that. Why? Because emotion would affect your focus."

The emotion of how high you were, and the consequences of falling off, would affect your ability to focus on walking across it. Rather than focus on the board, you would focus on how high you were. It is still wide enough, and anyone in the room could have walked across it if they could have focused. The width of the board is not the issue; one's focus is the issue. Circumstances affect our emotion, and emotion affects our focus.

Coach Landry was always able to control his emotion and stay focused on the objective, regardless of the circumstances facing him. I believe Coach Landry could have walked across a two-by-six laid across two twenty story buildings. He never focused on his circumstances. He just focused on the objective.

That is the type of focus he displayed on the sideline and modeled for his team. Coach Landry was always in control. He always collected his thoughts and focused. His players saw that, and followed his lead. The team consistently found a way to block out the distractions of any particular situation and stay focused on team objectives. That was one of their biggest strengths, and it helped the Cowboys win games.

Players look to their coach and respond to their coach. Coach Landry made this a point of emphasis for him. He used to say, "Leadership is a matter of having people look at you and gain confidence, seeing how you react. If you are in control, then they are in control." This was certainly the case with the Cowboys.

That is why the Cowboys always played with such confidence, because they were an amazingly focused team. They had great leadership, and their leadership helped the team stay focused on their objectives.

Following the lead of their coach, collectively as a team, they were able to control their emotion and direct their energy toward accomplishing team goals. When you watched the Cowboys, they always looked like they were in control. Even when they were losing a game, they still looked like they were in control.

That was a big part of why they were able to come back and win so many games. They never panicked, and they never quit. In football, uncontrolled emotion will often tempt you to do one of those two things when you get down. But the Cowboys did not allow that to happen.

Like their coach, the Cowboys as a team always seemed to be cool, calm and collected. Nothing seemed to rattle them. They rarely allowed the emotion of the game to affect them. They almost always kept their composure, and that is not always easy.

With so much emotion being a part of football, it is difficult at times to control it. Emotion has the ability to get you down and discouraged. It has the ability to be a distraction to your focus. It can cause a detour of your direction. Emotion can get you all out of sync. But as an individual player, and as a collective team, you cannot allow that to happen. You have to be able to control your emotion. The Dallas Cowboys had a unique ability to do that.

The Dallas Cowboys controlled their emotion in difficult circumstances and that helped them win a lot of football games. Every season is filled with highs and lows and the Cowboys were able to stay focused through both. Their ability to stay focused helped them become one of the most successful franchises of all time.

Lesson Learned

In life, at times you have to be able to look past your current circumstances and focus on your intended future destination. You cannot be derailed by a moment of emotion. You have to be able to take charge of every situation.

When I react in emotion, many times my actions can have negative consequences. In moments of frustration, I have to keep my eye on the prize. My goals are my pursuit.

Having the ability to control my emotions allows me to consistently move toward my goals. I need to keep the big picture in mind at all times. I cannot allow someone or something to push me off course. Controlling my emotion allows me to make the best decisions in life.

Life Exercise

1. Read the Quotes at the beginning of the chapter. Reflect on them, and then write down the thoughts they bring to your mind.

2. Ask yourself these questions: what type of job do you do in the area of controlling your emotions? Do you allow moments of emotion to push you into poor decisions? Do you allow other individuals or other circumstances to push your buttons? Do you react or do you respond? Do you fly off the handle or are you able to calmly and wisely respond?

3. Take the time to develop more self-control. Make a decision to not allow certain people or certain circumstances to pull a negative, unproductive response out of you. Take control of your emotion and take control of the situation.

For The Record

During Tom Landry's best 20 years, the Dallas Cowboys were in a position to go the Super Bowl 12 years. Here is a comparison to the Cowboys best twenty years without Coach Landry.

Dallas Cowboys   1966 – 1985   12 Championship Games

The Dallas Cowboys were one game away from the Super Bowl 60 percent of the time.

Dallas Cowboys   1991 – 2010   4 Championship Games

The Dallas Cowboys were one game away from the Super Bowl 20 percent of the time.

In the end, as a fan, all you can hope for is that your team has a chance to make it to the Super Bowl. You cannot fault the Oakland Raiders for the "Immaculate Reception" the Steelers pulled off against them, and you cannot fault the Minnesota Vikings for losing on a "Hail Mary" against the Cowboys. Games can change on one play. Ultimately, as a fan, you just want your team to be in the thick of things on a consistent basis. Coach Landry provided that for Dallas Cowboy fans for twenty consecutive seasons.

D.D. Lewis 51

50 Linebacker

Spent 12 years playing for the Dallas Cowboys

D.D. Lewis starred at Mississippi State University from 1965 to 1967 as a two-way player and three-year starter. Lewis earned All-Southeastern Conference honors twice and was a first team All-American selection his senior year.

Repeatedly anointed as the top linebacker in the Southeastern Conference, Lewis made a distinct impression on rival coaches. Hall of Fame coach Bear Bryant called D.D. Lewis "the best linebacker in the country". Bill Yeoman applauded Lewis' ability to recover and pursue, and said that he was the finest linebacker he had seen that year. Following the 1967 season, Vince Dooley said he was the best linebacker Georgia had faced, adding, "He's terrific."

Lewis won numerous awards: SEC all-sophomore team (1965), All-SEC (1966-67), SEC defensive player of the year (1967), UPI-All American (1967), and outstanding athlete (1968). Lewis was inducted into the nation's College Football Hall of Fame in 2001

Lewis was drafted by the Cowboys in 1968. In 1973, after serving as a backup for four seasons, Lewis took over the weak-side linebacker position when Chuck Howley retired, and held this position for eight straight years.

To this day, he holds the Cowboys' playoff record with 27 games played. During his NFL career, Lewis played in 12 NFC Divisional Contests, one NFC Wild Card Contest and nine NFC Championship Games. He made five Super Bowl appearances, winning Super Bowl VI and Super Bowl XII. During the 1980 season, he and Larry Cole, became the first three-decade players in franchise history.

Lewis wore #50 and played for 13 years, until his retirement after the 1981 season. He was voted the "Most Popular Player" by Cowboy fans and was given the Bart Starr Meritorious Award in 1981.

Although he was never selected to a Pro Bowl or All-Pro squad, he served as defensive co-captain in 1977 and 1978. In 1984, he was named to the Cowboys' Silver Anniversary Team. He started 135 consecutive games, which ties him for third place in team history.

He is one of only eight NFL players who have played in five Super Bowls: (V, VI, X, XII and XIII).

Number 19

Find Your Encouragers

Flatter me, and I may not believe you. Criticize me,
and I may not like you. Ignore me, and I may not forgive you.
Encourage me, and I will never forget you.
—*William Arthur Ward*

Nine tenths of education is encouragement.
—*Anatole France*

Taking an interest in what others are thinking and doing is often
a much more powerful form of encouragement than praise.
—*Robert Martin*

One word or a pleasing smile is often enough to
raise up a saddened and wounded soul.
—*Therese of Lisieux*

Correction does much, but encouragement does more.
—*Johann Wolfgang von Goethe*

A word of encouragement during a failure is worth
more than an hour of praise after success.
—*Unknown Author*

I can look back at my own life and see where a
few words of praise have changed my entire life.
—*Dale Carnegie*

Encouragement

That which imparts courage, inspiration, and motivation; that which energizes, stimulates, lifts up, gives strength to and support to another.

Find Your Encouragers

D.D. Lewis Interview:

For the Cowboys, the encouragement we were able to find from our coaches and from one another was a significant part of our success. There was a great deal of encouragement within the Dallas Cowboys' organization. We stood behind one another. We encouraged one another. That encouragement helped us to consistently push through adversity and a find a way to win.

Some people have the wrong idea about our coaches and our locker room. It is true that the Dallas Cowboys were all business, and no one would have ever described Coach Landry or his staff as "rah-rah" coaches. At the same time, our coaches did understand the value and necessity of timely words of encouragement.

The same was true of our locker room. While no one would have viewed our locker room as an on-going pep rally, what we did have was an environment of encouragement which helped us believe that we could do anything. That is what encouragement does; it helps you believe you can do anything you put your mind to. It is difficult to describe what it is like to be a part of a locker room where everyone is supporting one another. You really have to experience it to understand it. I haven't experienced anything like it anywhere else.

Without a great deal of encouragement, my career would not have amounted to much of anything. The fact is, without encouragement I don't think I would have even made the team. I was in serious need of encouragement from day one, as I faced some long odds of making the squad my rookie year in 1968.

The truth was, I didn't know if I could play in the NFL. I never thought I was all that great in college. I just thought the public relations guys pumped me up and made me sound better than I was. So when I didn't get drafted until the sixth round by the Dallas Cowboys, a team that was already loaded with talent, and I realized they had drafted two linebackers in front of me, two guys who were both faster than me and bigger than me, I sincerely doubted my chances of making the team..

To make things worse, when training camp arrived, I started off on the wrong foot. The first thing everyone had to do at training camp was run the infamous Landry Mile, which I wasn't ready for. I was out of shape. I had not been working out, and I was not ready to run the mile.

When I started running, it did not take me long to realize I was not going to make it all the way through. When I got a little past half way, I knew that one of two things were about to happen. Either I was going to pull up or I was going to throw up, but I was not going to finish the mile. I decided to pull up. I told the coaches I pulled a muscle. It definitely was not the first impression I wanted to make. Thankfully, after practice, Coach Landry did allow me to have a second chance at running the mile, and I was able to complete it.

My performance at the beginning of training camp was terrible. My first month of practice and our first scrimmage that year against San Francisco was a nightmare for me. I was horrible. Especially in the scrimmage, where I had hoped to show I could play against competition. That did not happen. I hadn't learned the defense yet.

At the time, I was playing both ways: center on offense, linebacker on defense. With the responsibility of learning both positions, I had fallen a little behind on defense, and that day I simply didn't do anything to help myself make the team. I walked away from that scrimmage feeling really bad about myself and my chances of making the team. I was down; I never would quit, that just wasn't in me, but I was down and close to being out.

Every day after the San Francisco scrimmage, I expected to get cut from the team. I just knew my days were numbered. I knew that if I did not start making some plays in practice, then I was going to find myself packing my bags to go home. What I needed desperately was some confidence. Making plays is all about confidence. You have to have confidence in your ability to make plays.

Fortunately, I received some encouragement from my cousin, John Raggio. John called me all the time. From the day I was drafted by the Cowboys my cousin kept telling me I was good enough to play in the NFL.

It was the weirdest thing. Every time I found myself at a low point, I found myself getting a call from my cousin John. If it had not been for him telling me over and over again, "you can do this, you can do this, you can do this," then I may have lost confidence in myself all together.

By the grace of God, his words allowed me to hold onto hope. They helped me to keep fighting. His words of encouragement gave me the confidence I was in need of at that time. That is what encouragement does; it gives you confidence in a time of need.

My cousin's words of encouragement gave me some confidence going into a new week of practice. I knew I needed to find a way to make some plays. Somewhere, somehow, I needed to get the coaches' attention. So I focused on every drill. One day, to my surprise, during seven on seven team drills, everything came together.

Out of the blue, all of a sudden, I flat-out dominated. I do not know what got into me, but I had one practice where I made every play. I am not bragging, I am just saying that day they could not block me, and I was making every tackle. I was making big hits, right and left. All the players and coaches were going crazy. I was trying to get the coaches' attention, and that day I got everyone's attention.

After practice, while I was in the lunch hall, Coach Landry came up behind me and spoke some words to me that changed my life. He came up to me said, "It is about time you started doing something, that is what we have been expecting from you."

Those were powerful words. Some may not see it as much, but for me, it was everything. It was only a few words, but it was not the number of words that mattered. What mattered to me was that Coach Landry took the time to speak to me at all, because he did not have to.

Coach Landry did not have to say anything to me at all, but he choose to. He went out of his way to do it. And with the few words he spoke, he communicated volumes to me.

For me, it let me know he cared. It let me know he noticed. It let me know he already thought I was a good player. He must have, since he had been expecting me to make plays. It let me know that he believed in me. That may be the most powerful thing of all about encouragement; it lets you know that others believe in you.

Coach Landry didn't spend a lot of personal time with his players, but when needed, he did find time to speak words of encouragement. Coach Landry's words of encouragement changed my perspective. His words inspired me, motivated me, and empowered me. It was a pivotal moment for me.

I remember when something similar happened to Charlie Waters. Charlie Waters, who was one of the best safeties in the league for much of his career, had one particular game against the Rams where he was forced into action as a cornerback.

It was a difficult day for Charlie, to say the least. Charlie was beaten three times for touchdowns, and those touchdowns were a big part of our loss. After the game Coach Landry addressed the team and spoke directly about Charlie and his difficult day.

Coach Landry said, "You know Charlie had a rough game today, and a lot people are going to hold him responsible for our loss, but if I had forty-five guys who played as hard as he did, we would not lose a game." Charlie said that Coach Landry had his heart from that moment on. Obviously, that moment encouraged Charlie, but it also encouraged all of us. That is the type of coach we had. We had a man who stood with us and supported us in our most difficult moments.

My most difficult moments were during training camp my first year; but after that one day of practice and that vote of confidence from Coach Landry, I became convinced that I could play in the NFL. Sometimes it does not take a lot. Even a few words of encouragement can dramatically change your outlook. From that point on, I believed I could play in the NFL. Now, I just needed to find a way to make the team. Right about that time I received a piece of advice from an unexpected place.

In the middle of training camp, I was asked to play in an All-Star game in Chicago. Every year, some of the best players from the previous college season would go and play the past year's NFL champion, which that year happened to be the Green Bay Packers. I got invited to play at the last minute because someone got hurt. While I was up there I ran into Ray Nitschke, the Hall of Fame linebacker of the Green Bay Packers.

Ray took the time to share some thoughts with me, knowing I was a rookie trying to make the Cowboys. He told me I needed to focus on one thing. He said to forget about everything else and just focus on one thing: special teams. Get on as many special teams as you possibly can, and make the team that way. That was his advice. He said that was how he made the Green Bay Packers. So that became my plan. I thought if it worked for him, then it could work for me. I appreciated Ray taking time to give me that advice, because it encouraged me as well. It gave me hope. It gave me something to focus on.

When I got back to training camp, I was a new man. I had confidence, and I had a plan. I also had the support and encouragement of the veteran players. Once they saw that I could make some plays, they realized that I could contribute to the team. I felt like they got behind me and encouraged me on another level. It is not that they hadn't supported me before, but once they saw what I could do, they wanted me to do that every time. They encouraged me to play up to my potential.

The Cowboys had just begun winning, and the veteran players were looking to win some more. They were looking for guys that could come in and help them continue to win. If you had the potential to do that, then they wanted to see you play up to your potential. The Cowboys had lost a lot of games their first five years, and the veterans did not want to lose anymore. The previous two years before I got there, they had lost each year to the Packers in the playoffs. They were close games. The Cowboys were close to winning it all, which was their goal, and they were determined to find a way to get it done.

They had a great group of leaders that set the tone for everyone else. Everyone was all about the team. They understood that you won as a team, and you had success as a team. They wanted everyone on the team to do as well as possible. Everyone encouraged one another. Everyone encouraged the other to be the best that they could be.

It is something I have always missed outside of my time with the Cowboys. I miss having a group of individuals who were so genuinely concerned about my own success. I miss having a group of individuals who encourage me to do as well as I possibly can. I miss having a group of individuals who encourage me to accomplish all I have the ability to accomplish. I miss all that. All of that contributed to my success.

I made the team my rookie year and played for the Cowboys for fourteen years. People often ask me, "What was the highlight of your career?" They usually guess it was my two interceptions in the 1975 NFC title game against the Rams. But I always tell them that the highlight of my career was making the team in 1968.

It is easy to get discouraged in the NFL, especially when you are a rookie trying to make a team as talented as the Cowboys were in 1968. I needed all the encouragement I could get. Discouragement always stands in the way of achievement. I believe encouragement is the greatest means of overcoming discouragement. I am grateful for the encouragement I received from my coaches. I am grateful for the encouragement I received from my teammates. They encouraged me, and I made the team. We encouraged one another and we won two World Championships. Encouragement was a vital part of everything we accomplished. Encouragement was a vital part of our success.

Lesson Learned

Anytime you attempt to accomplish anything of any significance in life, you are going to face discouragement. As D.D. Lewis said, discouragement always stands in the way of achievement. Discouragement attacks your confidence by questioning your own ability. Discouragement tries to keep you from reaching your potential and fulfilling your purpose. Discouragement tries to convince you to quit.

Encouragement is the greatest means of defeating discouragement. Encouragement gives me the courage to continue to pursue my goals and dreams. Thus in my pursuit of success I need to create my own environment of encouragement. I need to surround myself with people who inspire me with hope and provide me with help. When others believe in me, it makes it easier for me to believe in myself.

The reality is that attaining success in life is difficult, and I need all the encouragement I can get. The majority will tell me that I can't. I need to take the time to find the few who will remind me that I can.

Life Exercise

1. Read the quotes at the beginning of the chapter. Reflect on them, and then write down the thoughts that they bring to your mind.

2. Ask yourself these questions: Do the people you spend the most time with encourage you? Do they believe in you? Do they motivate you? Or do the people you spend the most time with ultimately hinder you? Do any of

them discourage you? Do they allow you be something less than you're best?

3. Make a decision to surround yourself with people who encourage you. Remove yourself from those who hold you back. Take the time to find real friends, individuals who always have your best interest in mind; those who want to see you fulfill your full potential.

For The Record

While most believe that Tom Landry's record of twenty consecutive winning seasons will never be accomplished again, here is a list showing where current NFL coaches stand. Bill Belichick, who has many similarities to Coach Landry, is currently atop the list.

Tom Landry	1966-1985	20 Consecutive Winning Seasons
Bill Belichick	2001-Present	11 Consecutive Winning Seasons
Mike Tomlin	2007-Present	5 Consecutive Winning Seasons
John Harbaugh	2008-Present	4 Consecutive Winning Seasons

It is difficult to believe a coach would stay with the same team for twenty plus years in this day and age, but Bill Belichick has a chance to do so. Belichick does three things well that Tom Landry did well: he drafts well, he develops well, and he deals well. A coach has to do well in the draft, he has to be able to develop players, and he has to make good trades and do well in free agency.

Mike Ditka

81 Tight End

Spent 12 years as a player and a coach for the Dallas Cowboys

Mike Ditka is widely regarded as one of the best tight ends in college football history. He was an All-American his senior year, and he went on to be enshrined in the College Football Hall of Fame.

Ditka was drafted in the first round, fifth overall of the 1961 NFL draft. He played five seasons with the Chicago Bears, earning Rookie of the Year honors and a trip to the Pro Bowl each of those seasons.

Ditka ended up in Dallas, finishing his playing career and beginning his coaching career. Ditka spent 12 years combined in Dallas as a player and a coach. He helped the Cowboys win a Super Bowl as a player and a coach.

George Halas brought Ditka back to Chicago in 1982 as Head Coach of the Bears. Ditka led the Bears to the playoffs seven out of the eleven years he was in Chicago. The Ditka-led 1985 Chicago Bears are regarded by many as being the greatest NFL team of all-time. That 1985 team only lost one game in the regular seasonand went on to win the Super Bowl, destroying the New England Patriots.

Mike Ditka was inducted into the NFL Hall of Fame in 1988. Today, Mike Ditka owns resorts and restaurants, among other things, and is an NFL commentator. He is one of the most well-known celebrities in sports.

Number 20

Never Quit Persevering

Great works are performed not by strength but by perseverance.
—*Samuel Johnson*

I do not think that there is any other quality so essential
to success of any kind as the quality of perseverance.
It overcomes almost everything, even nature.
—*John D Rockefeller*

Perseverance is a great element of success. If you only knock long enough
and loud enough at the gate, you are sure to wake up somebody.
—*Therese of Lisieux*

Perseverance, secret of all triumphs.
—*Victor Hugo*

Football is like life - it requires perseverance, self-denial,
hard work, sacrifice, dedication and respect for authority.
—*Vince Lombardi*

Permanence, perseverance and persistence in spite of all obstacles,
discouragements, and impossibilities: It is this, that in all things
distinguishes the strong soul from the weak.
—*Thomas Carlyle*

Persevere

To hang in, to hang on, to remain steadfast and immovable; to persist in anything you take on; to proceed, maintaining a purpose in spite of difficulty, obstacles or discouragement.

Never Quit Perservering

Interview with Mike Ditka:

The reason the Dallas Cowboys had so much success under Tom Landry was because neither he nor his teams ever gave up. Coach Landry was a fighter, and his teams were made up of fighters. There was no quit in those Dallas Cowboys football teams. Quitters never win and winners never quit, and the Dallas Cowboys were made up of a bunch of winners. They persevered through difficult times and enjoyed a great deal of success of because of it.

The Cowboys always kept fighting. They always kept working. They always kept looking for a way to win, and in the end they did win a lot of games. The Cowboys had confidence in themselves because of the amount of work they had put into the preparation process. Many times the Cowboys came back and won games in the fourth quarter because they were in better shape than the other team. The Cowboys had a great deal of mental toughness which served them well late in games.

Under Coach Landry, the Dallas Cowboys were always mentally tough. You become mentally tough by preparing to win and refusing to lose. That is mental toughness. You are mentally tough when you are willing to do whatever you have to do in order to win and when you simply refuse to give up.

Mental toughness is about persistence and perseverance. Mentally tough people never give up or quit, they simply regroup. I learned a lot about mental toughness when I went to Dallas.

My life changed dramatically when I met Coach Landry. My perspective changed about many things, and I became a better person and a better player. Coach Landry did things right. Coach not only talked the talk, he walked the walk. He was a living example for all of us of what a man and a Coach should be.

In Dallas, I grew as a person and a player. It was no longer about me. It was no longer about individual statistics. It was all about the team. In Chicago, I was counted on to catch the ball and score touchdowns. In Dallas I did a lot more blocking. In Dallas I did whatever Coach needed me to do.

That is the type of player you had to be for Coach Landry. Everyone on that team was interested in one thing, winning. Nothing else mattered. Individual statistics certainly did not matter. Everyone was interested in doing whatever we had to do to win football games.

Anyone familiar with the Dallas Cowboys knows they did not get off to a great start as a franchise. In their first six years, they did not win a lot of football games. It wasn't until year seven as a franchise that they had their first winning season.

There were a lot of people who saw Coach Landry as being a failure. There were a lot of people who were ready to write off Coach Landry and the Dallas Cowboys. But Coach Landry and the Dallas Cowboys never quit working to get better.

No amount of adversity could have kept Coach Landry and the Dallas Cowboys from becoming a winning franchise. They had players and coaches with too much character and too much heart. Regardless of what they were faced with, they were going to keep pushing forward.

Giving up would never be an option or consideration for Coach Landry. He had too much fight in him for that. He was driven and determined. No amount of difficulty, doubt, or discouragement could have ever convinced him to quit. It was never a question of whether or not he would be successful; it was only a matter of when.

Coach Landry did things the right way, and when you do things right, then it is only a matter of time before you become successful. Coach Landry did not waver. There was no in between with him. He had his convictions, and he lived by them. He was a man of great faith, and his faith would allow him to persevere through anything. Nothing fazed him. You could not rattle Coach Landry.

Coach Landry knew that even though at times things could look bleak, they could change in an instant. That was the case for me when I went to Dallas. Before I received a call from Coach Landry, things were looking a little bleak for me and my future. Then everything changed.

In 1968, after a terrible year in Philadelphia, I thought my career was over.

I really did. I had played eight years in the NFL, and I thought I was probably going to end up back in Pittsburgh tending bar telling old football stories for the rest of my life. Then, to my surprise, the Cowboys traded for me.

Coach Landry traded for me at a time when no one knew if I could play football anymore, myself included. But Coach Landry gave me a shot. He believed I could still play. He felt that he knew the type of player and person I was, and he believed I could still be successful.

You have to hang on. Persevere through the difficult times, because you never know when your life will drastically change. My life changed when I went to Dallas. Everything opened up for me. Again I went from thinking I was going to tend bar for the rest of my life to playing in a Super Bowl. In Dallas, I played in a Super Bowl and I coached in a Super Bowl. My opportunity to be a Head Coach, where I won a Super Bowl, came as a result of me going to Dallas.

Before Coach Landry gave me a shot, I didn't see a lot of career opportunities being presented to me. But when Tom brought me to Dallas, the course of my life was altered. That is the truth. I cannot emphasize this enough. You can never quit. Never give up hope. Never quit persevering. Persevere through it all, because you never know when things will change.

Keep persevering. Keep fighting. Keep battling. Never give up hope. Keep doing things right, and you will find success in life. The worst thing anyone can do is quit. To give up is the worst thing you can do. It does not matter how far down you are; you can comeback. Under Tom Landry, the Dallas Cowboys always believed that, and because of it, they put together twenty consecutive winning seasons. Keep fighting, keep doing the things you need to do, believe that things are going to change, and they will. Some people quit when success is right around the corner. Don't be one of those people. Don't quit until you have accomplished everything you wanted to accomplish.

Lesson Learned

Success does not happen overnight. And rarely is success achieved without facing a great deal of adversity. Coach Landry and the Dallas Cowboys did not have success right out of the gate. They didn't win any games their first year and didn't have their first winning season until year seven.

But a lack of success early on is no reason to quit pursuing it. You have to persevere through the difficult times, regardless of how bad things look. You have to stay focused on doing the necessary work and have faith that things will turn around. They did for Tom Landry and the Dallas Cowboys.

Quitting is never an option. Setbacks and failures are a part of life. All I can do is to keep learning, keep working, keep improving, keep doing the right things and keep believing that success is on the way. I reap what I sow in life. If I sow the principles of success into my life, then I will reap a harvest of success. I will hang on in the hard, dry times and push through to accomplish the goals I have set for my life.

Life Exercise

1. Read the Quotes at the beginning of thechapter, reflect upon them and then write down the thoughts they bring to your mind.

2. Ask yourself these questions: How do you respond to adversity? Do you have a tendency to quit? Are you willing to give up when things get tough? How determined are you to fight through difficult times?

3. Make a decision to never allow doubt, difficulty or discouragement to alter your course in life. Refuse to give up on your goals and dreams. Hang on, regardless of how bad things look. Persevere and overcome.